AF594113

The meditation techniques included in this book are to be practiced only after personal instructions by an ordained teacher of Life Bliss Foundation (LBF) or Nithyananda Vedic Sciences University (NVSU). If some one tries these techniques without prior participation in the meditation programs of LBF or NVSU, they shall be doing so entirely at their own risk; neither the author nor LBF nor NVSU shall be responsible for the consequences of their actions.

Published by Nithyananda Vedic Sciences University Press
(A division of Nithyananda Vedic Sciences University, USA)

First Edition: Dec 2005

Second Edition: Jan 2008

ISBN 13: 978-0-9790806-7-8 ISBN 10: 0-9790806-7-3

All proceeds from the sale of this book go towards supporting charitable activities.

Printed in India by Adwit India Pvt. Ltd., Bangalore. www.adwitprint.com

Discourses delivered to Swamis and Ananda Samajis of the Nithyananda Order all over the world.

Beyond Life and Death

PUBLISHED BY NITHYANANDA VEDIC SCIENCES UNIVERSITY PRESS
A division of Nithyananda Vedic Sciences University, USA

Unless one learns to overcome the fear of death, one cannot learn to live and enjoy life...

A seeker approached an enlightened Zen master, and asked, 'Master, does an enlightened man speak?'

The master replied, 'A truly enlightened person can never speak. Enlightenment cannot be expressed in words. An enlightened person can never speak and if he speaks, you can be sure he is not enlightened.'

The man then asked, 'Oh! An enlightened person is always silent then?'

The master said, 'An enlightened man can never be silent. If he keeps mum, be very clear that he is not enlightened; because if one possesses enlightenment, one cannot keep quiet. But in enlightenment, we can never possess it, only enlightenment can possess us.

If we possess something, we can keep it under our pillow or put it in our treasure box. But when enlightenment, when God possesses us, we can never be silent. So if somebody is silent, you can be sure he is not enlightened.'

The disciple was naturally confused, and asked, 'But, what is the truth? You say that an enlightened master never speaks, and then you say he never keeps quiet. Then what is the truth? What does he do?'

The Master says beautifully, 'He sings.'

About this book

Death is the beginning, not the end. It is celebration, not mourning. It is liberation, not the finish line.

One who realizes this truth is enlightened.

Time and again, great masters have taught how to live life by understanding death. If one does not understand what death is, what the process entails, how one goes through the process and what lies at the end of the process, it is impossible to be aware of how to live one's life.

In a series of three discourses, Paramahamsa Nithyananda takes us through the journey of death, as he has experienced it. This journey is one of timeless truth.

> 'It has been said that no one who has died comes back to tell the tale and no one who tells the tale has really died. On the contrary, every master who is enlightened has gone through the process of death, has traversed its path and has returned out of sheer compassion and love for fellow humans to tell them what he has experienced. We only need to listen to their song.'

- Paramahamsa Nithyananda

CONTENTS

What More Do You Want?

A small story from the great Hindu epic, the *Mahabharata:*

There was once a king by the name of Yayati. He lived extremely well for a hundred years, enjoying his kingdom and all the physical and mental comforts of life.
At the end of one hundred years, Yama (God of Death) came to take him, as it was time for him to leave planet Earth.
The king was shocked to see Yama and started crying, 'Why have you come so fast and suddenly, without any notice? I have not lived my life fully yet! Please, give me some more time to live!'
Yama replied that no extension was possible to one's span of life.
Yet, Yayati pleaded with him and begged him for more time.
Yama finally conceded that if any one of his sons was ready to give his life for Yayati, then he could live for that much more time.
Yayati was happy.

He called one of his sons and said to him, 'Please give up a part of your life and give me more time to live.'

The son was dutiful and fond of his father. He gave up the remainder of his life and died instantly.

Yama granted Yayati another hundred years to live.

Yayati continued to enjoy all the material comforts in the same manner as before and lived another hundred years.

At the end of this period, Yama returned to take Yayati.

This time too, Yayati felt he had hardly lived his life.

He begged Yama saying that he was not prepared to die yet and wanted more time.

Yama gave him another chance.

Another of Yayati's sons gave up his life for his father, and Yayati's life got a lease of another hundred years.

Now after Yayati enjoyed the next hundred years, Yama came back to take him.

Again as before, Yayati asked for more time, but Yama refused to oblige him this time.

Instead of agreeing to Yayati's plea as before, this time, Yama asked Yayati compassionately, 'Great king! Do you think you can put out a fire by pouring oil into it? Do you think you can fulfill your desires by living them out more and more?'

In just a few beautiful words, Yama explained the whole purpose of life to Yayati.

The *Mahabharata* says that Yayati, at that moment, experienced *Lakshmi* (Goddess of wealth) in his being. You may note that the Mahabharata does not say Yayati experienced Saraswati (Goddess of Learning); it says he experienced *Lakshmi* (Goddess of wealth). *Lakshmi* here does not symbolize outer world wealth; it symbolizes the richness of the inner world and the enhanced quality of life because of that. He finally realized the truth, followed Yama and rested at the feet of the Divine.

The quality of our life does not depend on the quantity of our wealth or our possessions. If this were so, then all the rich and wealthy people, the so-called successful people, would enjoy the highest quality of life. But if you just ask around, you will come to understand that it is not so.

There are many people who have failed to achieve what they want in life and as a result suffer from discontent and the feeling of failure. We may think that people who have been successful in being able to get whatever they wanted in life should be contented and fully satisfied. On the contrary, many times we see the strange situation where people who have achieved everything - material and emotional in life, still feel dissatisfied. These people suffer from 'depression of success'.

It is true that we need wealth to enjoy life, even to lead what we may call a reasonable standard of life. But we may have all the wealth we want in life and still be discontented. Wealth as such, does not fulfill one. There is a deep driving need within us that goes beyond material possessions and acquisitions. There is a part of all of us deep within that we are not even aware of, which keeps telling us that there is a purpose to our life which is beyond material success. The discontent that arises out of this is what I call 'depression of success'. But most often, we don't diagnose this feeling properly, and suffer because of this.

When we fail in our attempt to achieve something, we have the hope that the next time, we will be able to achieve success. So with depression of *failure*, at least there is the hope that keeps us going in life. However, if we have already achieved everything and we are still not satisfied, there is nothing that can give us satisfaction through the material world. Depression of success has no cure in further acquisition, either material or emotional. We need to understand that we have to raise the quality of our life. That is the only action that will bring us true happiness and true wealth.

The story about the origin of *Lakshmi* is also representative of this fact: when the ocean of milk (the mind) was churned by the *devas* (gods) and *rakshasas* (demons), using the *Meru* Mountain as a fulcrum and the giant serpent *Adi Sesha* as a rope to churn, from deep inside the ocean, *Lakshmi,* the Goddess of wealth emerged. This is actually a metaphorical representation: when the mountain of pure awareness churns the ocean of milk, that is the mind, it raises the quality of our lives in the form of *Lakshmi*.

Most of us think that our minds are very logical. Actually, the mind is most illogical. Just try this experiment: sit down for five minutes and write down all the thoughts that come to your mind in these five minutes honestly without editing. Then, read what you have written and you will realize how illogical your mind is. We are running a mental asylum inside our heads! One moment, we might have been thinking about our workplace, then, for no particular reason, we find ourselves thinking about our house. The next moment, without realizing it really, we might be thinking of our children. There is no connection, no rationale and no logic in the way our mind moves from one thought to another. The association of thoughts is highly illogical.

And we have entrusted our whole lives to this mind of ours. Can we imagine the nature of the mind to which we have entrusted the entire control of our lives? Vivekananda says, 'The mind is like a drunken monkey that has been stung by a thousand scorpions.' Just imagine the state of this monkey! Our mind is like this monkey that just jumps madly with no control over itself! The mind is not under our control; we are under *its* control.

I have studied the working of the mind of thousands of people by asking them to write down their thoughts, unedited, the way I have just now described. When I analyzed these outputs in detail, I found that in the majority of the cases, what we may refer to as the average human, there was a commonality running like a thread. The commonality was: eighty percent of their thoughts were based on greed and fear. These thoughts, these desires and fears, were in fact controlling them. The interesting part was that they were not even aware of this. It was the unconscious part of their mind that was generating these thoughts of greed and fear. The unconscious mind was not only generating these thoughts but also actually deciding what was to be done in their lives.

A small story:

> *There was a man who had just bought a new car after learning how to drive.*
> *He was very eager to go around town and so started driving it.*
> *He started the engine and drove for sometime and gained speed.*
> *Soon, he lost control of the car and the car went all over the road in a zig zag fashion and crashed into a tree and stopped.*
> *A friend who came to his rescue asked him in surprise, 'Why are you driving the car when you don't know how to drive? And that too such an expensive car!'*
> *The man replied, 'What do you mean I don't know how to drive? Of course I know how to drive; I just don't know how to stop!'*

Most of us are in a similar situation like this man who knew how to get the car to move but did not know how to stop it. He was not driving the car; the car was driving him! Similarly, most of us are not in control of our minds; our mind controls us. Be very clear: the mind is just a collection of all our thoughts. So if we lack clarity in our thoughts, it only means that we are having too many contradictory thoughts crowding in our mind.

But somehow, we are happy just being caught in the contradiction of our thoughts, unproductively. There is a popular saying that goes: if you make people think they are thinking, they love you. But if you *really* make them think, they hate you! All our energy gets sapped in thinking unproductively. If we expended energy to make only productive and quick decisions, we can make 10 times more decisions in any given time. We have to get out of the unconscious zone of crowded thoughts and get into conscious thinking.

It is possible to move from this seemingly generic state of unconscious non-awareness, to a state of awareness and conscious thinking. When we reach this state of awareness, almost 90% of our thoughts are for universal benefit and self-healing. Our very presence will radiate positive vibrations. That is why when you sit around a master, you feel an unexplainable goodness and a longing to be there for as long as you can. The master is an embodiment of goodness because he is in a state of pure awareness all the time. When we internalize these concepts, our awareness too will increase and slowly our mental set-up will be generated anew. Then, what the master does at his level, we will do at a microcosmic level!

When we analyze clearly what is right and what is wrong, what is eternal, what is the truth, and what is not, from this analysis, intelligence will arise and our quality of life will increase. This feeling of fulfillment is what is referred to as *Lakshmi.* Goddess *Lakshmi* stands for wealth and richness, for overflowing, and for prosperity. All these refer not just to the material wealth but to the wealth of the inner world, to the inner richness. Real richness is not money, it is the quality of the being and of life itself.

Money can be got through any means. It is not a big deal. It does not require much. Just a few business techniques and greed for money is enough; you will become rich! But the inner richness is what we need to work for. It is the inner richness that is the real overflowing, the real prosperity.

Our house is filled with all kinds of comforts, with all kinds of things to make us feel happy and fulfilled, but our *being* is unfulfilled. Fulfilling our being is called *Lakshmitva,* having *Lakshmi* within us. Our mind always works towards having more and more. However, by its very nature, 'more' can never be 'fulfilling'. I can say, 'more' is the opposite of 'fulfilling'. But we always feel we need more to be fulfilled! That is where we miss the whole thing. Have you seen a single person who has been fulfilled by having more? Never! They only want more and more! So understand, the moment you ask for more to be fulfilled, you will *never* be fulfilled. Just see what you have with full awareness for a moment; then you will be fulfilled!

We always travel in the horizontal dimension of 'what next'? 'What next'? Sankara (an ancient enlightened master) says beautifully that the mind is like a musical instrument that continuously plays *tata kim, tata kim* (what next? what next?). As long as we are moving in this horizontal plane, we will run and run till we drop dead in our grave. Greed is what really drives us in life. If it is not greed it is fear. Either this or that.

A small story:

> *An eminent doctor successfully cured a sick child.*
> *A few days later, the child's mother called on the doctor.*
> *She first expressed that his services were of the sort that could not be fully paid for. She paid her deep gratitude for what he had done and continued, 'But I hope you will accept as a token from me this purse which I myself have embroidered.'*
> *The doctor replied very coldly to the effect that the fees of the physician must be paid in money, not merely in gratitude, and he added, 'Presents maintain friendship, not a family.'*
> *'What is your fee?' the woman inquired.*
> *'Two hundred dollars,' he replied.*
> *The woman opened the purse. There were five $100 bills. She took them out, put back three, and handed over two to the doctor and left.*
> *The doctor sat alone and self-conscious.*

Greed drives our thoughts, words and actions. We therefore fail to recognize the beautiful things in life. We are blind to the beautiful things. We see only what is there in everything for us. We miss because of this. We are in a hurry to travel in the horizontal direction. Traveling from more to more is only traveling towards our grave. It can never be life; it is just slow death.

Another small story:

A man was sitting in a bar, drinking. He noticed an old lady from the Salvation Army going from table to table, advising people not to drink and to clear their lives of bad habits.

He tried avoiding making eye contact with her, but still she came to his table and started saying, 'Don't you realize that you are consuming slow poison?'

The man, who was already irritated by her preaching replied, 'I know. But I am not in any hurry!'

The idea of more and more is also slow poison: traveling towards death. It will never allow us to taste life. It will never allow us to enjoy life, to totally and truly relax. If we have a deep satisfaction, we will enjoy life. If not, the greed for more will enjoy us. To a certain level, *we* drink alcohol. Then, *alcohol* starts drinking us. Up to a level, *we* smoke tobacco, after which *tobacco* smokes us. Up to a level *we* eat food, after that *food* starts eating us. If our life is based on craving, if we move on the horizontal line continuously, it will be a never ending process.

We need to understand that there is one more dimension to existence, to our life and to our being: what I call the vertical line. When you travel in this line, you start living the reality that you have; you start enjoying intensely what you have. This will give you an immensely deep satisfaction and reveal a whole new space, a whole new dimension of life. Instead of going for more and more to enjoy, your enjoyment will increase with what is already there.

Most of us think that we crave for things because we enjoy them. No! If we are sensitive, our consciousness expands and we will only enjoy and never crave. When I say enjoy, I mean enjoy what is there as reality, what is there in front of us. If I really enjoy this chair I am sitting on, I will not crave for a more sophisticated sofa. Just think: if we can enjoy this chair, will we be even thinking of the sofa? No! We think of the sofa only because we are dissatisfied with the chair. The thought of the sofa itself will not surface in our range of consciousness if we are happy with the chair! And when we don't have the mindset to enjoy the chair, be very clear, we will not have the mindset to enjoy the sofa either, because the problem is not with the chair but with the mind. If we cannot sleep on an ordinary cot, even a queen size bed will not satisfy us because once we get it, we will start dreaming about a king size bed! You may say, 'No, no, how will we think beyond a queen size bed?' But I tell you, it will happen. It is happening to you in so many other ways already, if not with the example of the queen size bed.

If our mind set is trained towards a philosophy of 'more and more', a new layer which psychologists call the cerebral layer opens up, where we start enjoying things mentally but not physically. This layer stores all our fantasies and when we enjoy, we enjoy thinking of those things, and not the things that we really have. We just mentally enjoy, that's all. If we have a Lexus, our cerebral layer will be enjoying a Benz. When we get the Benz, our cerebral layer will already be steering the wheel of a Rolls Royce! This way, we continuously escape reality.

In today's society, we are continuously living in the cerebral layer. If we feel like dancing in a public place and we cannot, since society does not permit us to do so, what do we do? We satisfy ourselves vicariously by watching people dancing on television. Why do you think there is so much pornography around? Youngsters enjoy sex through watching it, that's all; just mental enjoyment.
At least with physical enjoyment, there is an end. When we get tired, we will stop dancing or stop enjoying or stop watching. But with mental enjoyment, where is the end? We can keep on enjoying the dance visually in our mind and we will never get tired! That is why this is so dangerous. Two things happens when we mentally enjoy. First, as we continue to watch and enjoy, we accumulate more and more fantasies from what we see, and second, we never get fulfilled through it.

People ask me, 'Master, what is renunciation? Should I renounce the world to become enlightened?' I tell them that there is no need to renounce anything that you have. Just renounce what you don't have. What we have is not a problem: it is ours; we should enjoy it. Renounce what you don't have. We are trying to continuously enjoy what we don't have through fantasizing. Renounce that! That is what I mean when I say, 'Renounce what you don't have.' That is what craving is.

Enjoying reality never disturbs one. It is only the ghost of craving that troubles us. In Sanskrit, there is a beautiful word called *maya*, which cannot really be accurately translated to English. *maya: ya ma iti maya* (that which is not there is *maya*). That which is not there, but which troubles us as if it is there, is what is *maya*.

When we fantasize about a super model or Miss World, immediately, our wives seem ugly. Be very clear that the outer woman never disturbs us. It is only the inner women who disturb us. Reality never creates trouble; only when we try to convert our fantasies to reality does the trouble begin.

Let me tell you a small story which I repeat very often in my discourses:

There was once an old man who used to go to the beach regularly in the evenings, sit on the sand, and watch people walking.
A curious young man who had seen this old man coming everyday to the beach and sitting there for hours walked up to him and asked him why he was doing this.
The old man replied, 'I am in search of my perfect life-partner.'
The young man was shocked. He asked him, 'How long have you been in search of her?'
The old man replied, 'Since I was twenty-five.'
The young man was surprised and asked if he ever came across a single woman who met his expectations.
The old man answered, 'Yes, I did meet her some years ago.'
The young man asked, 'Then what happened?'
The old man answered, 'But then she was in search of the perfect man!'

Drop your fantasies, your imagination about what you don't have.

We pick up these ideas from the media, advertisements, television and movies - about the best eyes, nose, mouth and lips, and start yearning to have these for ourselves. Then, our body starts looking imperfect, even ugly to us. The billion-dollar cosmetics industry is thriving, thanks to this acceptance by us to base our self-esteem on their ideas of a perfect body. We start hating, consciously or unconsciously, this beautiful gift of our body bestowed on us by Existence. When we do this, we create a deep wedge, a deep wound in our being.

God is not an engineer to mass-produce the same type of beings. He does not have a mould to turn out identical clay dolls. He is an artist who creates unique pieces of art in His creations. Each of us is as unique as every one of His unique creations. If we understand this, we will love our bodies. And when we love our bodies, we stop asking for more.

Living Within our Boundary: Living in the Present

When we drop the idea of having 'more and more' and start living in the present moment, we start living inside our boundary. What do I mean by 'start living inside one's boundary'?

We get up in the morning and while we are brushing our teeth, we think about the office. When we reach the office, we begin making plans for the evening: to go to the beach or maybe to a restaurant. In the evening, we go to a restaurant, but once we are there, we are already thinking about going home and resting. Similarly, on a Wednesday at the office, we start thinking about the weekend. But when the weekend actually arrives, we start worrying about what work needs to be done in our office on Monday. On Monday, we are already thinking about the next weekend! By living in this fashion, we tire out very easily!

One thing is for sure: if we are here, our mind is not here. Our mind never stays where our body stays. This is the life style of 'more and more'. We run, run and run, without even knowing what we are running for. It is a rat race. In a rat race, even if we win, we are still a rat!

When we run with all our energy, we forget to enjoy, we forget to live. We forget to have *Lakshmi* in our life. Again, it is the quality of our life and not the quantity that is important.

The other life style, where we live inside our boundary, where we live in the present moment, creates a new mental set-up: what *Vedanta* calls a cognitive shift; we start to live more intensely, with awareness, what Buddhists call Zen, mindfulness. Our living is then centred in our being; we feel fulfilled. We are always in bliss. Life opens a new dimension.

We feel continuously dissatisfied because we are under the continuous threat of our desires. We need to understand the term: threatened by desires. Observe carefully: the moment a desire arises, there is a deep uneasiness in our being, body and mind. If the desire is fulfilled, we start worrying about whether we will get to experience the same joy again or not. On the other hand, if our desire is not fulfilled, there is a hangover, a deep craving to fulfill the desire. Not only this, often we experience guilt the moment our desires get fulfilled. Until the desire gets fulfilled, there is greed. The moment it gets fulfilled, there is guilt! This is the usual pattern we trace with desires.

When craving enters our being, it splits our being into two halves. One side of our being craves the desired results, while the other side works towards fulfilling the craving in reality. This is what is schizophrenia. One half is thinking about what should happen, while the other half of us is living the real life. This gap between reality and imagination is what I call tension.

There are two kinds of lifestyles: living with 'more and more' and living with 'this and this'. Either we enjoy this or nothing, now or never!
There are only two kinds of mental set-ups: that of a man who enjoys the path as well as the goal, and that of a man who enjoys neither the path nor the goal. Be very clear: we can never enjoy only the goal unless we choose to enjoy the path first, because the path itself is the goal. This is a very deep concept which if understood can turn our lives around by 180 degrees.

For example, when we are young, we yearn to settle in America, thinking that life there will be good. When we get there, we start working on buying a good house, thinking we will be happy after that. Once we get the house, we think that after marriage, life will be good. After marriage, we start feeling that when we have children, they will give us happiness. After having children, we start worrying about them and imagine that when they grow up and settle down we will finally be able to retire with money, be free from worries, and enjoy life.

However, by the time we retire, the mental set-up we have created to continuously run behind 'more and more' becomes a habit. We forget the art of enjoying life. Relaxation is only a word for us, not an experience. Naturally, we have lost sensitivity to life, the quality of enjoying life. It is like selling your eyes to purchase a beautiful painting; selling your sleep to buy a bed; like selling your life to purchase a house!

Krishna says emphatically in the *Bhagavad Gita*: *karmanye vaadhikaraste maa phaleshu kadachanah* (do your duty, but don't expect results.) This verse is often considered the essence of this timeless scriptural work - *Bhagavad Gita*. Krishna does not mean that we should work without expecting our salary. What He means is, let the job itself become the enjoyment. Let the path itself give us bliss. When we enjoy the path, even if we fail to get the desired result, we will feel deeply satisfied. However, if we do not enjoy the path, even if we succeed, we will feel only dissatisfied.

When we postpone enjoyment, when we postpone living in the present, when we constantly hope to live in our future, the habit of postponement becomes a mental attitude. Be very clear: whatever we may acquire in terms of quantity, it is the *quality* of our life that gives it meaning. We may have a beautiful bed, but it serves the purpose only if our mind can sleep on it. So work to increase not the height of the bed but the depth of your sleep.

A small story:

> *There was once a forgetful man who used to continuously keep a reminder of what he needed to do.*
> *Once, he had to remember to do three tasks and as a reminder to himself he tied three knots in his handkerchief.*
> *He finished two of the three jobs but could not remember the third job however hard he tried.*
> *He sat up the whole night racking his brains, trying to remember the third job.*

Just as dawn broke, he suddenly remembered the third job that he had tied the knot for: to remember to have a good night's sleep, since it was the weekend!

This is how we waste our whole life. We plan to enjoy but never actually enjoy ourselves. If the quality of the mind is not present, what is the use of getting a weekend to enjoy our vacation? We will be in a different place but if we are carrying the same restless mind, the attitude is still the same.

A man came to Buddha seeking assistance to cure him of unhappiness in his life.

There was nothing exceptional about it; many others faced the same difficulties.

He seemed to have had an endless succession of small disappointments and complaints.

He was a farmer and he enjoyed farming. But sometimes it didn't rain enough or it rained too much and his harvests were not the best. He had a wife and she was a good wife whom he loved. But sometimes, she nagged him too much and sometimes he got tired of her. He had children and they were good children. He enjoyed them a lot. But then life was never stable; it was an unpredictable roller-coaster. And of course life is that way!

Buddha listened patiently to the man's story until he finished. He looked at Buddha expectantly, waiting for some word to fix everything.

Buddha said, 'I can't help you.'

The man was startled. He said, 'I thought you were a great teacher! I thought you could help me!'

'Everybody has got problems!' said Buddha. 'We always have eighty-three problems, each one of us, and there is nothing we can do about it. If we manage to solve one problem, it is immediately replaced by another. We will always have eighty-three problems. We are going to die, for example. For you, that is a problem. And it is one you cannot escape. There is nothing you nor I nor anyone else can do about it. We all have problems like this and we never seem to be able to free ourselves from it.'

The man became dejected and exclaimed, 'Hey! what good is your teaching?'
'Well,' said Buddha, 'It might help you with the eighty-fourth problem.'
The man asked, 'The eighty-fourth problem? What is the eighty-fourth problem?'
The problem that we don't want any problems!' said Buddha.

If we can free ourselves from our desire to be free of our difficulties, then what difficulty do we really have? As to what happens to us in life, we may have little or no choice. But as to how we deal with it, we have total choice. Why don't we exercise that?

The moment we create sensitivity in our being, even water tastes like *amrita* (nectar). There is a *sutra* (technique) in the *Katopanishad* that says, 'If we give away all our things in the *Vajpeya yagna* (sacrifice), we will become *Indra* (king of Gods). The underlying meaning of this *sutra* is that if we sacrifice the idea of craving, of having 'more and more', we will be in a different space. We will have the sensitivity to live and enjoy what we have.

A beautiful story from the life of Buddha:

> *There was a king by the name Aparasanjita whose wife was related to Buddha.*
> *From a very young age, the queen had been associated with Buddha and knew Him.*
> *She continuously inspired the king to meet Buddha at least once.*
> *Finally, the king decided to go meet Buddha.*
> *Being a rich and powerful king, he did not want to go like an ordinary person and decided to take the best diamonds with him to give to Buddha.*
> *The queen warned him that Buddha would not accept diamonds and suggested taking flowers instead.*
> *So the king decided to take both flowers and diamonds.*
> *In one hand, he had a chest full of diamonds, while in the other hand, he had a plate full of flowers.*

When he arrived, he saw Buddha seated with His ten thousand disciples seated in front of Him.
He proceeded towards Buddha.
Just as he was about to offer the diamonds, Buddha said, 'Drop it!'
The king was shocked, but since he was in front of ten thousand disciples, he quietly dropped the diamond chest and proceeded with the flowers
towards Buddha.
Just as he started walking, Buddha said again, 'Drop it!'
Surprised, the king dropped the plate of flowers, feeling really stupid in front of the big crowd.
When the king now took a few steps forward, Buddha said again, 'Drop it!'
The perplexed king was not able to understand.
A senior disciple of Buddha who was standing and watching what was happening said, 'Buddha is not asking you to drop the diamonds or the flowers. He is asking you to drop the idea of having 'more and more'. The diamonds are not even worth dropping; drop the idea that these things have value. If you feel that diamonds have value, you will fear the idea of dropping them. That is why Buddha asked you to drop the false idea of what is valuable, what is great. He is not asking you to drop physical things. He is asking you to drop your cravings. He is asking you to drop your mind, your ego.'

So understand: neither running after 'more and more' nor leaving outwardly comforts will help us; only drop the idea of having 'more and more'.

Bring your mind to the present moment, to live life from moment to moment. Then, life will become joy, bliss and ecstasy; you will live life more intensely, with consciousness and awareness. Whatever you do, do it totally and completely. If you are drinking water, drink it with totality. If you are eating, eat it with complete awareness, totally. Whatever you are doing: walking, driving or sleeping, do it with full consciousness and awareness.

A king once went to a Zen master and asked him, 'Master, I have heard that you always live with joy and bliss. What is the technique that you use to do so?'
The master replied, 'When I eat, I eat. When I sleep, I sleep.'
The king was confused and asked the master, 'Do we not do the same thing?'
The master replied, 'Surely not! When you eat, are you really eating? You plan for the future, worry about the past. When you eat, eat. When you sleep, sleep. Then your whole life will become worship. If you live life with the attitude of having 'more and more', life will be like work. If you live with the attitude of 'this and this', your life will be worship.'

Understand one thing clearly: either our whole life can be work or our whole life can be worship. We cannot have part-time work and part-time worship. Whether our life is work or worship depends on our attitude. With the right attitude, work becomes worship. With the wrong attitude, even worship becomes work. When we see priests in temples and other places of worship mechanically going about their jobs, often for commercial reasons with no passion, no compassion and no devotion, we can understand how even worship can turn into drudgery.

With the right attitude, anything can be converted to meditation, to worship. With the wrong attitude, even meditation will be converted to work. Going intensely into anything with absolutely no attachment to the results is the way to convert work to meditation. One more thing that has to happen here is a deep awareness about the core in you that is lying undisturbed inside although you are continuously working outside.

Once a disciple went to his master's cottage and came out after some time, crying.
After some time, another disciple entered the master's cottage and came out laughing.

The first disciple was surprised and asked the second one, 'I asked Master whether I could smoke while meditating and he beat me. What did you do? What did Master tell you?'

The second disciple said, 'I asked Master if I could meditate while smoking! And he said OK!'

There are different attitudes for any action. Here, one attitude resulted in a disciple getting beaten and the other attitude resulted in a disciple getting praised.

Our attitude decides our life. With the right attitude, we are showered with more and more. There is a beautiful *sloka* (verse) in the *Puranas* (sacred text) which says, *nanda* (bliss) attracts fortune. There is one more saying, 'Where there is bliss, *Lakshmi* (Goddess of wealth) walks in naturally.' This is not just a simple faith or belief. Even modern-day psychologists say that if our mind is blissful, we attract happy people and happy situations around us. If we are sad and depressed, we attract the same type of people and incidents, sad and unhappy, causing us more sadness and unhappiness.

The being is like a dish antenna. If we tune ourselves to joy, we attract bliss; if we tune ourselves to depression, we attract suffering and pain. Our being always attracts like incidents.

Be very clear: we can either enjoy this moment now or never! Tomorrow is going to come to us as today. So if we postpone our enjoyment today in the name of tomorrow, we will postpone it tomorrow in the name of day after tomorrow. It is our choice.

If we understand what life is, we will understand that we don't need anything. We are not just given what we need; we are actually showered. However, if we don't understand this, however much we are showered with, we will take life for granted.

A small story:

There was once a small boy, who was begging for alms in front of the king's palace. The king on seeing him felt pity for him and offered to let him stay in the palace guest room for a couple of days.
The boy was very happy to be in the palace; he had a sumptuous meal and went with great curiousity to his room.
On reaching the room, he was disappointed to see a medium-sized room with a small bed and some other furniture. He was expecting a royal room with servants waiting on him, with the choicest of foods and a big and royal bed.
He lay on the bed, muttering about how a palace could have such a mediocre-looking room, and finally went to sleep.
The next morning, the king enquired how he was doing, to which the boy could not help expressing his dissatisfaction at how he had been treated and how the room was not up to his expectations.
The king was furious at the boy's audacity and ordered his guards to throw him out.
The boy was thrown out of the palace. He started walking, weeping profusely.
On his way, he met a Sufi master who was begging for alms.
The master asked him why he was crying and the boy told the master how he had been invited to the king's palace and was not given fair treatment and was ultimately thrown out.
The master asked the boy to accompany him back to the king's palace. So the boy covered his face in case the king recognizes him and accompanied the master.
On reaching the palace, the king saw the Sufi master and the boy, and invited them with all respect, to stay in the palace for a couple of days.
The master profusely thanked the king for the offer, had a great meal and was taken to his room.
He was given the same room the boy had been given earlier and they both spent the night in that room.
The next morning, the king inquired of the master how his night had been.
The master expressed deep gratitude for the excellent treatment and thanked him for the royal room and the comforts.

The boy could not believe what the master was saying.
The king was overjoyed and handed the master a thousand gold coins and offered him the guest room to stay in for as long as he wished.
The Sufi master thanked the king once again profusely and went on his way.

The same situation gives rise to entirely different reactions and events! It is the attitude that makes the difference. When we live with the attitude of gratitude to Existence for all that it showers us with, life will shower on us and everything will become beautiful and we will live it to the fullest.

What More do you Want?

What more do you want? Let us understand this statement first.

A small story:

One man decided that he should pray as hard as he can to God so that he may live the life he has been dreaming of for all those years.
He was a rich businessman but he was driven by a deep desire to have much more.
God appeared because of his perseverance in prayer.
The man could not believe that God had appeared.
He asked him, 'God, how much is a penny worth in heaven?'
God replied, 'One million dollars.'
The man then asked, 'How long is one minute in heaven?'
God replied, 'One million years.'
The man asked, 'Can you give me a penny?'
God replied, 'Sure. Just wait a minute!'

When we get greedy, when we start asking for more and more all the time, God knows how to take care of us!

When we understand how much life showers on us, we will understand: what more do we want? If we don't understand what life has showered on us, even in our grave we will be complaining that our neighbour's tomb is better than ours!

Don't be cheated by the mind which tells you that you are an ordinary person with ordinary blessings. One important thing: to become a Picasso or a Ravi Verma, we need talent and we need intelligence. However, to become enlightened, we do not need talent or intelligence; just our 'ordinariness' is more than enough. We need this understanding, that's all.

Ramana Maharishi once said, 'The moment you say that I am *Bhagavan* (God) and you are ordinary, you have missed my teachings.'
We hide our ego in a beautiful way by saying that we are ordinary. If the mind accepts the fact that whatever I say is always easy to practice, you should immediately start practicing my teachings. I never tell impractical things. But for you to practice my teachings, your mind has to die; it has to lose its grip on you. Like all other beings, the mind also has its own instinct to survive. That is the reason it does not allow you to go about without worrying about the past or the future.

With just a little intelligence, we can reason whether worrying has helped us solve a single problem in the past. If we have ten problems to start with, we create the eleventh problem of worrying about the ten problems. We cannot be so poor in our understanding. It is like saying, 'I understand fire burns, but I cannot resist the temptation to put my hand in the fire!' It is that foolish!

If this one point is understood, the very attitude of worrying will disappear from our system. I read a few lines about worry the other day. It said:

In this life there are only two things to worry about.
Either you will be rich or poor.
If you are rich, there is nothing to worry about.
But if you are poor, there are only two things to worry about.
Either you will be healthy or sick.

If you are healthy, there is nothing to worry about.
But if you are sick, there are two things to worry about.
Either you will live or you will die.
If you live, there is nothing to worry about.
If you die there are only two things to worry about.
You will either go to heaven or to hell.
If you go to heaven, there will be nothing to worry about.
If you go to hell, you will be so busy shaking hands with all your friends, you won't have time to worry!

In a very jovial way, this conveys the truth about why we need not worry. If you read this, you will understand that there is no need to worry at all because not even an iota of good is going to come out of it; only our minds are kept unproductively absorbed in it.

People ask me, 'Master, I have tried very hard but my mind does not become silent. What can I do?' I tell them, you don't know how much work is going on inside your mind! There are scientists doing research on Artificial Intelligence (AI) and they say that to do $1/100^{th}$ of the work of data gathering, processing and analyzing that our mind does, we need a computer the size of a three-storey building and the noise generated will be as much as that of a large factory! The mind does so much work with no noise!

If we can put this mind of ours to productive use, and if we can use it as a tool at our disposal, we can do wonders with it. Instead of going behind unwanted thought patterns and conclusions, if we can understand that we can succeed with what we have, it is enough. Don't bother if you have failed nine times and succeeded only one time. If you have succeeded one in ten times, increase the number of trials to one hundred. You will succeed ten times, simple! If we increase the number of trials, efforts and struggles, naturally we will see more and more moments of bliss.

We are Not Ordinary

We can easily hide in low self-esteem. When we have high self-esteem, society kicks us; our ego is disturbed. If we have low self-esteem saying that we are ordinary, society will never teach us; it will only praise us, it will only praise our humility! But this is an easy and cunning way to protect our ego.

Never keep yourself in low self-esteem. I say, whatever esteem we have of ourselves, except that 'we are God', is low self-esteem, because we *are* divine! Don't think that you are just your mind; you are truly divine.

If we associate ourselves with moments of our success, our moments of success will naturally increase. Somebody was telling me the other day, 'Master, I am working on myself and I see the change happening slowly.' Be very clear: change is never slow; it is always quantum. Either we transform or we don't. Postponement is a cunning method the mind uses to escape.

We complain, 'I am a house-holder. I have so many things to take care of. How do I change? I am so restless; how can I meditate?' This is like saying, 'I am too sick. How can I take medicine?'

Understand this: if your mind is restless, it is then that you need to meditate. If you feel you are an ordinary person, it is then that you need these teachings. If you truly feel you are extraordinary, you don't need these teachings! If you feel ordinary, you need to practice with 120% effort.

When we begin to enjoy ourselves, we will express ten times the creativity that we express now. As of now, our minds are focused on the philosophy of 'more and more'. Eighty percent of our energy is therefore spent in *iccha shakti* (Power of Desire); only the remaining twenty percent of our energy is spent on *kriya shakti* (Power of Action). When we awaken *gnana shakti* (Power of Wisdom) in us, only 20% of our energy will be used in imagination, while 80% will be used in expressing our creativity.

In the great Hindu epic *Ramayana*, there was a character - Vali, who had the power to win away half the power of anybody who faced him in battle. Our desires are like Vali. When we face them in battle and struggle with them, we lose half our energy and power to them.

I am not saying don't build a big house or don't have a big bank balance; I am saying, drop the idea of having 'more and more'. Then we will be more creative, more productive, more energetic and more active and automatically we will have more! Running after 'more and more' is what I refer to as house-keeping in dreams. There is no use in house-keeping in dreams; do it in reality without the craving for it! The key lies in not craving for it.

Try this experiment for the next three days: just for the next three days, drop all your worries. Surely, by dropping your worries for just three days, you will not lose your job or house; you will not die either. So drop bothering about the future totally, utterly and stop worrying about the past incidents. Whenever your mind goes to the past or future, just break the words that come to your mind immediately and completely change the thought. Drop your cravings for just three days. If it does not work, you can pick up your cravings again. You don't have to believe in this also; just take it as a hypothesis and experiment for yourself. Decide consciously that you will not allow cravings, you will not run behind 'more and more' for the next three days. Don't plan on doing this eternally; you will never do it. Start with now, that is enough! You will see how active, fresh, creative, bright, full of life, energetic, and blissful you will become!

The moment we drop cravings, our whole energy becomes integrated and centred. Eighty per cent of it is available to express our creativity. As of now, eighty per cent of our energy is not working, since we are stressed out with subtle and gross desires. Once we realize this waste of energy, we will drop the idea of craving and it will automatically start getting used in creative work. We will start living in the vertical dimension of achieving rather than the horizontal dimension of running after 'more and more' and getting tired. We will start living in a different space.

Just try this experiment for three days; even if you lose something, it is worth trying. When we awaken the *gnana shakti* (Power of Wisdom), we start living intensely with awareness in the present moment. The mind is the supplier of energy. So if we are stressed out, how will we be creative?

J. Krishnamurti says beautifully, 'Ninety-nine per cent of our worries never come true and the one per cent that comes true is actually good for us.' The moment we remove the weight of worries from the mind, we remove the basic ingredients of stress; we will then see that we explode into energy and explode into creativity!

There is a wonderful statement by Mahatma Gandhi, 'We have enough to fulfill the whole world's needs. But, the whole world cannot fulfill a single man's wants.' Only a person like Gandhi can make such a statement. Gandhi's life was a living expression of this saying. He is truly one of the greatest human beings ever born on this earth. Apart from being a political leader, he had so many different dimensions to his personality. Only India can boast of having a leader who preached and practiced non-violence. All other countries boast of warriors as their heroes. Here is a man who died saying, 'Don't punish the person who killed me!' Even in the last moment of his life, he was concerned about others. Living religion is easy, but living religion at the moment of death is surely not easy. Gandhi was a person who lived his religion even at the time of death.

The world has enough to fulfill everybody's needs, but it cannot fulfill a single person's wants. In Jainism, there is a beautiful concept. I don't know whether it is a fact, but it is the truth. We need to understand the difference between truth and fact. Truths that are already discovered and already analyzed are facts. If a truth has been proven by some scientist, by a theory or analysis, it becomes a fact. There are so many truths though, which are yet to be discovered, yet to become facts. Just because a truth is not yet a fact, we cannot deny the truth. For example, before the theory of gravity was discovered by Newton, was there no gravity? Gravity existed before and after Newton discovered it; he only made it a clear theory and proved it to be a fact.

In Jainism, there is a truth that Mahavira states: When we come down to planet Earth, the total amount of food which we will eat is sent with us to planet Earth. The energy needed to fulfill all our desires is given to us when we enter Earth. The things which we are going to enjoy–our house, comforts, etc., are all sent to the world. The capacity to enjoy all our comforts is also given to us the moment we enter.

If this is the truth, why do we feel that we are lacking comforts? If I ask anyone whether they agree with this theory, most people will disagree saying, 'Oh, Master, God has given me less for sure. I don't think I received my share properly!' Most of us feel that something is missing; we feel deprived. But Mahavira says that all that we need has been already sent with us.

The problem is: after coming down to planet Earth, we see what others are enjoying and we start wanting to enjoy all that also; we start picking up desires from others. This is what we call borrowed desires. We not only want to work out our desires, we start gathering the desires of others as well. And we feel tortured that our desires are not getting fulfilled.

For example, we go to the mall to buy a refrigerator. There, we meet a friend who is buying a colour television and oven. Just a few moments before we met our friend, we were very happy buying the refrigerator. However now after meeting him we start feeling that we should also have the colour television. Our life was perfectly alright without the television until then. Even the thought would not have crossed our minds. But what has happened? From where did the desire enter? From where did the irritation about the television enter? Directly from the other person! This is exactly how we desire for more in every aspect of our lives, whether it is relationships or lifestyle or material things or anything.

Especially in lifestyle, we pick up a lot of things from others and start feeling the pressure to fulfill things.

The big problem is that we have enough energy to work out our desires in our life, but not enough energy to work out somebody else's desires as well in our life. We have one life. Hence, naturally, we have the capacity to live this one life's desires. If we add other's desires also in this life, the greed will result in stress. So we feel constantly that our time, energy and money are not sufficient; we feel deprived.

We have increased our desires after coming to this Earth. The energy which we brought is sufficient for our whole life. But when we start accumulating more desires and running after them, obviously the energy is not enough.

From a very young age, we are taught to compare. That is the reason we continuously compare and feel jealous. From young age, if there are 2 children in the house, we automatically compare the two of them in every situation and sow the seeds of comparison in them. Everything starts from home. We create sibling rivalry and then make efforts to sort it out. Straightaway, we damage their consciousness. If we can somehow avoid this comparison and labelling of children as grade a, b or c, we can eradicate more than eighty percent of the violence and misery on this planet. All violence starts like this.

People ask me, 'Master, if we don't have comparison, how do we grow; how do we progress?' I tell you: nobody can grow by comparing. Each being is unique; each being has to flower. If we compare, we may progress as the other person is progressing, but not in the way the individual in us wants to progress. It is a very wrong idea that we can grow only through comparison.

Some children are masters of visualization; they are naturally inclined to arts like painting, poetry, dancing etc. Some are masters of verbalization; they grow in the fields of logic and language. Some are more inclined to mathematics. There are different aptitudes and inclinations. But when we grade children, we generalize them without giving any credit to what they are and this is where the problem starts.

We expect children to excel in everything, to be perfect. I tell you, perfectionism is actually schizophrenia!

There was once a Zen master who announced a competition among his disciples to declare who maintained a garden in the best fashion.
The senior-most disciple was a perfectionist and he was known to clean the garden extremely well.
Everything was picture-perfect; all the old leaves were removed from the trees and the grass was mowed to be exactly the same height throughout the garden. The garden looked like a lego set. On the day of the competition, the master went around looking at the gardens of all his disciples. He went on rounds to inspect all the gardens.
When he came to the senior disciple's garden, he walked past it with hardly a glance at it.
The disciple was shocked and watched in disbelief as the master walked into the garden of the youngest disciple, next door.
The garden was nowhere close to as perfect as his, but it was maintained in a natural fashion, kept clean and tidy.
The master awarded the best garden award to this young disciple.
The senior disciple could not contain himself. He was angry and disappointed.
He asked the master why he was not given the best garden award.
The master just took a handful of old leaves from the young disciple's garden and scattered them in the perfect garden.
He then remarked, 'Now this looks like a natural garden.'

Understand, this story is not telling us that we should not sweep dry leaves in the garden. This is how we normally understand things. I am reminded of an incident that happened in the ashram one day:

The boys were called for a meeting. A senior ashramite started with the topic of keys missing because the boys were putting them in their shirt pockets and walking away. After a long lecture she asked, 'What do you think is the remedy for this? How can we prevent searching for keys all the time?' One mischievous boy replied, 'Hereafter we should not stitch shirts that have pockets!'

So the garden story does not mean that we should leave the dried leaves as they are. It is to make us understand that while perfectionism is needed in the outer world, it should flower out of a totality and not out of an obsession for it.

When we compare, we sow the seeds of misery. Naturally, this results in low self-esteem or high self-esteem.

Both low and high self-esteem are a problem. With low self-esteem, we get into a shell and suppress ourselves. We get jealous of the other person about whom we have a high esteem. If we have high self-esteem, our behaviour will be such that society will not support us. In both cases, we guard ourselves from society. We harbour violence in some form against society. The seeds of violence and misery are sown in our hearts at a very young age itself.

We continuously run based on comparison. So naturally, we pick up the attitude of violence; we pull other people down; we learn methods to stop the progress of others. The more we learn to compare, the more cunning and crooked we become. We hide ourselves behind cunning words like, 'How do we grow if we don't compare?'

The only way to escape from the torture of comparison and jealousy is to see that they are shadows with no objects. One glimpse of this truth will remove jealousy and comparison from our system.

A father one day turned off the light in his room and asked his son,
'How will you see things now?'
The son lit a candle.

They had light for some time but soon the candle melted.
The son lit another candle.
This candle also melted.
The father looked at him and said, 'Lighting the candle is of no use. Just open the door and allow light to flood the room. The darkness will automatically disappear.'

Candle light is only like temporary wisdom that saves the situation for us. Sunlight is what will permanently remove the darkness. Our ideas of jealousy and comparison are like the darkness that will disappear only if we bring the light of understanding into it. With understanding that they are not real objects, they can leave us forever. There is absolutely no scope to compare anybody with anybody. It is the most foolish thing to do. Each one is unique with a different agenda; then where is the scope to compare?

The truth remains the same. When we start to compare, we pick up desires from other people. We try to work out many more desires than what we can in our one life.

There is a beautiful *sutra* in the *Upanishads*: *Iccha Shakti* (Power of Desire and Creativity), the energy which creates desire in us, is potentially powerful enough to create *Kriya Shakti* (Power of Action), to actually fulfill this desire created in us.

For example, if we have the desire to possess a house, the very desire can express enough energy to create the house in our life. It seems to be a very strange theory, but the *rishis* (enlightened masters) declare with conviction, since we are God; if we have the desire, we have the power to also fulfill it. The *Brihadaranyaka Upanishad* says: as our desires are, so is our will; as our will is, so are our actions; as our actions are, so is our life.

Then why do we feel that we are not able to fulfill what we want? It is merely because we don't work to fulfill *our* desires only; we also work to fulfill somebody else's desire.

The next question comes up: how do I find out whether the desire is mine or somebody else's? The answer is: if the desire is yours, when the desire arises in you, the very desire will give you joy. When you fulfill the desire, it will give you a deep sense of fulfillment. If it is somebody else's desire, the very desire will cause a sense of uneasiness. Even after fulfilling the desire, it will leave a sense of hang-over, possibly guilt.

What is the difference between junk food and good food? With junk food, we feel filled but not fulfilled. With good food, we feel a deep fulfillment. After having junk food, we feel lethargic and feel like resting. This is strange: we eat to get energy but after eating, we feel like resting; we feel deprived of energy. After having good food, we not only feel satisfied, but we also feel energetic and ready to take on the next job.

Be very clear: if our desires make us feel tired, give us an uneasy feeling, cause disturbance in our mind, then there is something seriously wrong in our system.

According to the *Upanishads*, desires are energy. We cannot even move an inch without the desire to do so. Desire is the basic energy of our life. Without desire, we cannot get up from our seat now and leave.

If we observe ourselves, early in the morning, we enter our physical body from our dream body, either because we have a deep desire to enjoy something through our body, or because we fear that we will lose something. We think that if we don't get up and go to work, we will lose our job. The thought may not take shape exactly in this form, but that is the underlying insecurity, driven by fear or greed, that causes us to get up from our bed. Our desire to enjoy is the force which pushes us inside our physical body from the dream body.

Be very clear: we assume this human body just to fulfill our desires. So when we assume this human form, we bring enough energy with us to fulfill those desires as well, to unfold our desires as well.

Understand one more important thing: basically, our energy cannot do anything with partial involvement; in a half-involved manner. The moment we create a desire, we create and release the energy to work it out. If we feel unable to release that energy, then understand that it is not your desire; you have borrowed the desire from somebody else. Borrowing desires from others makes you dull and depressed.

There are four levels of desires. Let me explain each of these. The first level is the physical level: the desire for physical pleasures and comforts, the desire to see beautiful things, desire to hear, desire to taste, desire to smell and the desire for sex. These are the basic pleasures which form the first level of desires.

The next level is the desire for name and fame, for attention from others.

The third level consists of spiritual desires: the desire to be spiritual, the desire to have *darshan* (vision) of God and the desire for enlightenment.

The fourth and the ultimate, but very subtle desire is to just hang on to the body.

Analyze your desires deeply to see where you have need and where it is merely greed. If we analyze our mind, our lifestyle, we can classify our desires under these four categories. Whatever may be the desire, we can classify it under one of these four categories. Understand whether your desires are coming from need or greed. If it is your desire, it is need; if it is somebody else's, it is greed.

We have enough energy, power and capacity to fulfill our desires, but we don't have enough to fulfill the desires of others. Look in all the four layers of desires and identify all the layers where you are picking up others' desires.

The fantasies that we pick up from the outer world are what disturb us. Reality in life never disturbs us; our desires which we want to enjoy never disturb us.

People ask me, 'Master, should I renounce all my desires?' I tell them, no, that is also greed. We want to renounce here in the material world, so that we can enjoy in the future in the spiritual world.

I asked a person who used to drink regularly why he stopped drinking. He replied that he wanted to go to heaven. He had read that in heaven, we get *soma rasa* (drink of the demi-gods). So, he gave up drinking in this world, in the hope of drinking in heaven! I told him, never give up something on the basis of greed. Do it only on the basis of understanding. What is the guarantee that you will get *soma rasa* after death?

There are some sects of people who give money in this world to religious institutions. The priest gives them a receipt for the donation and promises that they will go to heaven through the power of their donation and the proof of the receipt. When the person dies and is buried, the receipt is placed along with the body. They believe that God will honour the receipt and give them the benefits of the good deed; they have an exchange offer with God!

If we drop things in this world in the hope of pleasures of the other worlds, remember it is still the same greed playing tricks on us. Look into your life deeply: in how many cases is greed replaced by beautiful words to describe it?

All our prayers are nothing but bargains. There was a man who was praying to *Lakshmi* (Goddess of Wealth), 'Oh, *Lakshmi*, please give me one million dollars. I promise you that I will donate a hundred thousand dollars to you then. If you don't believe me, you can deduct a hundred thousand dollars yourself and give me the remaining amount!'

Our greed has become an undercurrent in us. Another small story:

> *NASA was interviewing professionals to be sent to Mars. Only one could go and couldn't return to earth.*

The first applicant, an engineer, was asked how much he wanted to be paid for going.
'One million dollars,' he answered, 'because I want to donate it to M.I.T.'
The next applicant, a doctor, was asked the same question.
He asked for $2 million. 'I want to give a million to my family,' he explained, 'and leave the other million for the advancement of medical research.'
The last applicant was a lawyer. When asked how much money he wanted, he whispered in the interviewer's ear, 'Three million dollars.'
'Why so much more than the others?' asked the interviewer.
The lawyer replied, 'If you give me $3 million, I'll give you $1 million, I'll keep $1 million, and we'll send the engineer to Mars!'

This might sound funny as a joke but the truth is, greed shows up even in our humour. Our humour decorates our greed, that's all.

It is said that Lord Venkatachalapati in the temple at Tirupati in South India actually fulfills everybody's desire. Actually, it is a great enlightened master's energy that exists in that temple. There is a great spiritual energy existing there. Just like we can see whatever slide is projected in front of a projector as is, similarly, any thought comes to reality in front of Lord Venkatachalapati. The problem is: we pray and get into trouble since most of the time we don't even know what we need and what to ask for. He never misses; he always fulfills our wishes. But the choice of making the right or wrong wish is ours. Our desires are a projection of our greed. But we always find ways to try and hide and decorate our greed.

Our desires never make us feel tired, but living out the desires of others makes us feel dull and depressed. Have you seen any animal suffering from obesity? No animal suffers from obesity. Of course, pets may overeat and suffer because they pick up the habit from us. Have you seen animals getting headache or having to go to the psychiatrist?

Animals have plenty of food continuously available to them but they never overeat and suffer. Why? Because they work out only their own desires, never others'. In our lives, we pick up desires from others.

We are continuously exposed to advertisements of McDonald's and we pick up the desire to eat unconsciously. We are continuously bombarded by images and desires. We see a Starbucks, and the desire for coffee automatically arises; we enter the shop for coffee, irrespective of whether we need it or not. See at how many levels we exploit our body for the sake of our greed!

We always blame our body saying that because of our sensory pleasures, we have wasted our life. Never blame our senses or body. Our body is naturally intelligent. The problem is our mind. Never think that our body disturbs us; it is we who disturb our body. Just look at yourself; how many nights have you spent watching television when your body was begging for rest, but you stayed up watching a football or cricket match.

In India, a lot of Indians equate cricket with patriotism! Please understand: if your country, India, had to be represented, let it be represented by eleven enlightened masters, not by eleven cricketers! Cricketers cannot be representative of India and its culture. I am not against the cricketers. They are nice people but they don't represent India! If India has to be represented, let it be represented by Sankara, Ramanuja, Ramana or Vivekananda! Many countries may be represented by their players, since that represents their culture. These countries have universities and stadiums all over. But all over India, there are temples and ashrams; so the true representatives of India are the enlightened masters.

We torture our body for the sake of our joy. Even if our tongues are burning, we continue to eat spicy food. When our body feels comfortable with our desires, it is our need. If we are feeling tired even after fulfilling the desire, it is our greed. If we feel fulfilled after fulfilling the desire, if we enjoy, are in bliss, ecstasy, joy and if we feel we have flowered, it is our need. If we feel tired, disturbed or uneasy, it is our greed.

The second level of desires is the desire for fame. How do we know whether this desire is need or greed? Understand that attention is a basic need of our life. Research studies have shown that a man can go for ninety days without food and yet survive, but he cannot be mentally balanced for more than fourteen days without receiving somebody's attention.

We are all products of our society. Without human friendship and without the human smile, without human touch and interaction, our lives will become miserable. The loneliness will become intolerable.

If we are not attended to, loved and cared for, we feel something is missing. Attention is a basic need in everyone's life. Each of us wants to be loved, cared and attended to. But if it is just a need, we not only will have the desire but we will also reciprocate; we will automatically give others back what we get.

If it is greed though, however much we are attended to, we suck others energy and never feel like giving back and never feel that we have had enough either. We feel more and more powerful, but never feel like giving back the attention, the care.

We can see this very well in politicians. The more the crowd, the more is the volume of their voice and the number of promises that they make. The more energetic they are, the less is their service. Again, they work only for more attention and not to do something in reality.

Attention is also the basic reason for the existence of the family system. In marriage, we take multiple vows. One of them is the vow taken by both the man *and* woman: until the end of my life, I will support you whenever you feel the need for attention and care.

The problem is that nowadays, nobody knows the meaning of the vows that are taken at the time of marriage. It is more like the priest is getting married, rather than the bride and groom because it is the priest who chants everything. According to the Hindu system, there is no concept of divorce. We take the marital oath in front of *agni* (fire) that till the *jataragni* (inner fire of stomach) becomes cold (till we die), we promise to keep up the vows. So, it is a promise until death to support each other. So divorce is neither socially nor spiritually accepted in Hinduism. The man takes an oath to give all his attention, love and care to his wife and she in turn promises to give all her attention, love and care to him.

Marriages are supposed to be wonderful ways to exhaust each other's unfulfilled actions and not add any more to it. But today, marriages are endured on a different scale altogether.

> *A husband discovered that his wife always carried his picture in her handbag. He was thoroughly elated. He asked her, 'You always carry my photo in your handbag to the office. Why?'*
> *The wife replied, 'When there is a problem, no matter how impossible, I look at your picture and the problem disappears.'*
> *The husband exclaimed, 'You see, how miraculous and powerful I am for you!'*
> *The wife calmly replied 'Yes, I see your picture and say to myself: what other problem can there be greater than this one?*

This is how some of the marriages are endured today!

So understand, if we are really in need for attention, we will take the attention and also give it. The problem is again that we have the *greed* for attention.
In today's world, how long do you think one would allow his wife to watch her favourite television show without disturbing her? How long would a wife allow the husband to watch the news on television without pointing out how long it has been since he was glued to the television?

Be very clear: the greed of attention can never be fulfilled. Even if we get attention, we will constantly be in need of more. Why do people die to become celebrities? The greed for attention can take one to any extent, even to the extent of dying.

Before we get attention, we have a deep fear about whether we will get it. The moment we get it, we have a deep fear about whether we will lose it! Will our name and fame get spoilt in any way? Both before and after the desire, we are continuously in fear.

We may be in awe of celebrities, but understand that celebrities are actually like our slaves. Never think that our leaders are leading us; it is we who lead them. If you live near any celebrity, if you get to watch them at close quarters, you will understand how much of insecurity and fear they live with.

Without us, they cannot be celebrities! Their whole life and energy is based on our attention. But enlightened masters are not like that. We see: a *Paramahamsa* (enlightened master) is a *Paramahamsa* whether we are there or not. He does not need fans and followers. There are so many enlightened masters on planet Earth today who are living in bliss in caves in the Himalayas! But what about us? If we are a celebrity, we need fans to give us status. If we are a politician, we need citizens to follow us.

> *Once, a king after winning a series of wars, was feeling very powerful and proud. He was taking a tour of his kingdom, when he saw a man sitting under a tree, deep in meditation and blissfully unaware of the king's presence.*
>
> *He walked up to the man, angry that he had not even bothered to get up and salute the king. He drew his sword angrily and putting it to the man 's neck, threatened to kill him if he didn't salute him. The man started laughing loudly and asked him why he should salute the king.*

The king, now even more enraged replied, 'I am the king of this state! How dare you not respect me'! The man replied laughing, 'What kind of a king are you? You are begging for respect from me; you are no more than a beggar!'
The man under the tree was more like a king, since his self-esteem was independent of others' opinions of him. He did not need to beg for respect, for attention from others. The king was shocked at the statement and the body language of the man.

That is why it is said that when Buddha used to beg for alms, He used to look like a king and the kings like beggars! Outwardly, possessions cannot make us regal; it is the inner bliss that radiates and makes us regal.

Living each day as if it were to be our last, and living life to the fullest are the best ways to extract the maximum juice out of life and living. If you clearly understand the process and meaning of death, you can live life the way in which it has to be lived.

We do not have to wait till a death sentence is pronounced upon us to change our priorities and to question the way we live. Start today!

Understand: living in the now, welcoming reality, will take us to a different dimension where we will be able to use our creative energy to fulfill our true desires. Live every moment with total awareness. Enjoy this journey, this gift of life! This will automatically lead us to joy, bliss and ecstasy!

Mystery Of Mysteries

In the grand Hindu epic *Mahabharata*, the Pandava king Yudhishtra was asked by a demigod: what is the greatest mystery in this world?

Each of Yudhishtra's four brothers were stopped from drinking the waters of a pond that this demigod ruled, until they answered his questions.

Arrogant about their own powers, these princes defied the demigod, started drinking the water of the pond and fell down dead.

When Yudhishtra went looking for his brothers and found them all lying dead on the shores of this pond, the demigod appeared in front of him, and told him to answer his questions first before he drank his water.

Yudhishtra was known for his adherence to righteousness and he agreed to answer the questions posed by the demigod who owned the pond.

The question was: what is the greatest mystery in this world? Yudhishtra replied, 'The greatest mystery and the greatest wonder in life, as I have seen in my experience is this: thousands of people die everyday, and go to the abode of *Yama* (God of Death); yet, we people who are living here believe that we are going to live forever!'

The demigod, who was Yama himself in disguise, and in fact the father of Yudhishtra, was pleased with the sagacious response. He resurrected all the four brothers.

No one believes that he or she is going to die. People live with the idea that they will never encounter death. We always think that someone else can meet with an accident and die, but not us.

A lady was once telling her friend how egoistic her husband was. Her friend asked, 'Why do you say so? What did he do?' The lady replied exasperatedly, 'Instead of saying, 'When I die', he says 'If I die'!

This vital question about the greatest mystery of life elicits different answers from different people. Some say that birth is the biggest mystery, while others say it is death.

My very own experience of death matches the opinions of the *rishis*, and with the opinions of many who have had near-death experiences (NDEs). Death is the most mysterious of mysteries.

~ WHAT IS DEATH?

Our understanding of death can be broadly classified into two categories: there are people who believe in life after death and those who do not believe in rebirth. Of course, there are many who don't come under either of these two categories. They neither talk about death nor analyze it. They want to be deliberately ignorant. Their attitude is, let it come when it has to come, and we will handle it at that time. Why should we even think about it or discuss about it now? They prefer to take the escapist route.

In Western philosophy, there is no concept of rebirth. Their logical minds do not allow them to believe in it. There is no proof of rebirth. Even NDEs are only experiences of certain people. There is still an element of doubt about what death really is. Is it just the end of the physical body? Why does it really happen at the time it happens to every person? Many scientists are still working on this mystery. They have not been able to come to any decisive conclusion.

That is why in the West, people want to live their lives fully. They feel that they don't have a second chance to fulfill their dreams. So they are in a hurry to fulfill all their desires as soon as possible. This has created anxiety in man. This concept or belief of a single life is what has given birth to science. Man started to search for the maximum comfort, joy and juice from the outer world. Man wants to extract the maximum that he can at whatever expense to him and others during the limited period that he knows instinctively is all that he has in this world.

This belief of just one life has also given rise to the sense of purpose in life and the concept of God in the more serious and introspective humans. For most people, God is just a concept. They have not experienced Him. God is just a vague concept until enlightenment. In fact, even the idea of God was created only when the question of death was raised.

Many people have tried to answer these questions. In that process, they have created theories, philosophies and religions. Even the idea of God was created during this process only. The question of death is the most mysterious question according to me. From time immemorial, so many people have tried again and again to answer this question.

Every person who tried answering this question created a new religion, a new cult. All religions are born out of this question.

What actually happens after death? What is death? It is the most mysterious thing!

Let me answer this question first: why should we analyze death?
The answer is: our idea, our understanding about death, will change our whole understanding about life.

In Los Angeles, more than a hundred years ago, Vivekananda was asked by a young lady, 'What is life?' He replied, 'Come with me to

India and I will teach you.' She was confused and asked, 'What will you teach me?' Vivekananda said, 'I will teach you how to die!' It seems strange that the question was about life, but the answer was about death!

Actually, if we know the secret of death, our quality of life will be different! Our quality of life, our understanding and attitude to life will change.

Understand that death is not an incident that happens at the end of our lives. It is actually happening every moment of our lives! When the understanding of death permeates our consciousness, we will have a clear idea of life. We will realize that living and leaving are just two sides of the same coin.

Serious enquirers of the purpose of Existence in creating humans, eventually turned to the Eastern religions of Hinduism and Buddhism to resolve their doubts.

Eastern philosophy is based on the experiences of great enlightened masters and *rishis* (sages). They believed in many births. Instead of the limiting scientific tradition of the West born out of the limited space of life, the idea of unlimited space, time of life and death of the Eastern religions gave birth to spirituality. When we take birth again and again, enacting the same drama of a brother, sister, husband, friend and parent, we eventually feel tired of this drama. When we die, we leave these co-actors and move on. When we come back, we have a new setting. It goes on and on. After a while, we tire of going through the same cycle over and over. We look to be liberated. The moment we start thinking about liberation, we start thinking about *moksha* or enlightenment. Spirituality is all about this. Our understanding of death makes us understand life.

According to me, our concept of death is the one basis on which we live. There is a beautiful Zen saying, 'Learning the art of dying is learning the art of living.'

A Zen story:

> *An enlightened master once declared that he was going to die the next day at six in the morning. Of course, enlightened people know about their death. The disciples requested the master to wait for a few hours as it would be very cold early in the morning. That would also give them sufficient time for the funeral. The master, out of compassion, agreed to do so. He changed the time of his death to noon. Exactly at the stroke of twelve, he left his body.*

Enlightened masters truly embody Friedrich Nietzsche's words, 'Death of one's own free choice, death at the proper time, with a clear head and with joyfulness, consummated in the midst of children and witnesses, so that an actual leave-taking is possible while he who is leaving is still there.'

When the British were trying to establish their supremacy over India, they were very keen on taking control of a small village in Central India for strategic reasons.

There were only about a hundred tribal people living there (This village does not exist anymore).

The villagers were highly esoteric and mystical. They practiced meditation and it is said that they never fell sick. They were such highly evolved people that even if they hurt someone in their dreams, they would go and apologize to the person the next morning. They did not even want to harbour unconscious vengeance or hatred. They were a mature and spiritual group that had nothing of the outer world but everything of the inner world.

When the British tried to force their culture on them, they would not give in. They resisted. Even when they were threatened to give up or face dire consequences, they refused to do so.

They gathered in the centre of the village and right in front of the British soldiers, they chanted a *mantra* (chant) and dropped dead. Every single one of them dropped dead.

The soldiers could not believe their eyes. They had not anticipated that the villagers would commit suicide. This incident has been recorded by British soldiers.

They also said that for the first time, they felt guilty for being responsible for the death of such innocent, simple, yet great people. These people knew the art of dying. They could just drop their body and leave the world.

The *Bhagavad Gita* says, 'Death is just like changing your coat.' Learning to die is the one and only art that we are supposed to learn while we are living. There is a great fear of death, of the unknown, in most people.

A beautiful story from the *Katopanishad*:

There was a young seven year old boy by the name of Nachiketa.
He asked his father, who was a king, 'Why are people afraid to die?'
The king was irritated at what seemed to be an obviously understood fact. So, he scolded Nachiketa, 'Why don't you go face death if you are not afraid?'
Little Nachiketa was genuinely interested in finding out the answer and he set out to meet Yama (God of Death).
On reaching Yama's abode, he found that Yama was not there.
So he decided to wait.
After some time, Yama returned and he was shocked to see a little boy waiting for him.
All the time, Yama had to chase people, who in turn, tried their best to escape the jaws of death. And here was this small boy who had come boldly to face death himself.
Yama compassionately asked him, 'What have you come here for? You are one of the rare beings who has come to the door of death; normally people run away from me!'
Nachiketa replied, 'Master, that is what I have come to find out about. What is death?' Yama was surprised at the young boy's question. He saw the deep sincerity in the boy and gave him the Truth. Nachiketa became enlightened.

We see that Death is the greatest teacher! The teacher who can teach us enlightenment itself!

~ WHAT HAPPENS WHEN WE DIE?

Now, let us look into the mystery of death, which is truly the greatest mystery. Can anybody speak about death? In Tamil, there is a proverb, 'Those who have seen death have never come back.' Those who have come back have not seen it. No one can speak about death except an enlightened man. He is authorized since he has already undergone the death experience. He is dead. Unless we undergo death, we can never get enlightened, we can never get liberated. The mysteries of death can never be recorded or proved logically. They can never be reduced to facts and figures. They are such personal experiences, that only a few enlightened masters have spoken about them. Unfortunately, they have no certificates. God has not created a university or industry for enlightenment. Only a few who have had the experience share their views with others. Only a few who felt the energy of the master could take advantage of this science. That is why the mystery of death is unknown to most people.

This science can transform our lives. As we have not understood this mystery, we have missed so many things in life. The secret of death is not a very popular concept in the West because it can never be proved scientifically. Today, a lot of scientists and psychologists are researching accounts of NDEs. Thousands of people have experienced it. There is even a website which gives the experiences of nearly 10,000 people. We will be surprised to know that all their experiences are similar. Hypnotherapists adopt the regression method to know more about the past lives of the patients. Patients are hypnotized and taken back in life and lives, often resulting in information on past lives, how they enter into the body, and how and when they leave the body. We will see that the findings are very similar to what the *Upanishads* say about death. So now, this science is spreading in the West too.

What happens after death? We need a little bit of mental preparation before we can go in depth into this subject. Whatever I have spoken so far is only to prepare us, to bring us to a mental level from where we can understand what I am going to say. I promise you that what I am going to narrate about my experiences is the truth and the absolute truth. It matches the findings of the *rishis*, hypnotherapists, psycho-analysts and doctors. I developed that personal experience into a formula that will help people to overcome the pain at the time of their transition.

This is how this formula happened to me; this formula is behind the *Nithyananda Spurana Program* (NSP). I am trying to transmit and reproduce my experience as a master, just like a scientist develops formulae to reproduce the external truths that he observes.

I was in Varanasi, which is a sort of headquarters of Hinduism. Hindus are enjoined to visit Varanasi at least once in a life-time to wash away their sins by bathing in the sacred river Ganga that flows through this city. I was caring for an elderly monk of a particular religious order, who was sick. He was in the Intensive Care Unit (ICU), and I was sitting by his bedside.

This happened before my enlightenment experience. There was another person in that ICU ward who was dying. I could see the struggle of the soul leaving the body. The body was in tremendous pain, as if a knife was ripping across its entire length, as if a thousand scorpions were stinging him. The pain was so palpable that I wanted to run away from there; I could hardly watch. Suddenly, the being fell into coma; coma is a pain-killer; it is an automatic mechanism of the mind for the body to stop feeling the pain, that unbearable pain.

When I saw that being suffer, it seemed to last only for a few minutes, but for that being, it was eternal. The pain of that being remained with me; I too was suffering. I watched, but I could not do anything. The monk I was attending to recovered. A year after this incident, I became enlightened.

I travelled down to South India after my experience. Two years later, I was again in an ICU healing a disciple. This time too, another person was dying at a bed nearby. I saw that person die even as I was healing my disciple. I felt the pain starting; I wanted to run; but now instead of this being falling into coma and unconsciousness unable to bear the pain, it went into deep awareness - super consciousness! It was floating from one energy layer to the next and finally disappeared into bliss.

I asked the family of the dead man whether he was a very spiritual man, whether he was a great meditator or whether he was enlightened. They said no. He was a non-believer, an atheist, and not even remotely religious. I wondered how he could have had such a blissful death? How? Why? For this being, death was not an ordeal; it was a blessing. Why then did the other soul suffer a year back? I contemplated, I meditated. Suddenly, the knowledge that descended on me was the knowledge of what I now teach at the NSP. It is a science, a technology that arose from the experience of these two deaths.

All suffering is caused by memories of desires, the unfulfilled desires accumulated over births in our body, mind and spirit. NSP makes the inner space pure and clean; it dissolves all memories. It helps the the spirit leave peacefully, blissfully. Death becomes liberation and a celebration for one without memories.

When we leave the body, we cross seven different layers of our body: the physical, pranic, mental, subtle, causal, spiritual and finally nirvanic. As soon as we leave the body, as the spirit leaves the physical layer, we undergo a tremendous, unmanageable pain. A small cut in your hand gives you so much pain. Can you imagine what the pain will be when your whole body, your consciousness from head to toe is torn? The pain will be similar to the pain that one will undergo when stung by ten thousand scorpions at once! A little meditation while we are living will help us have a painless transition. It can heal and guide us at the time of passing away.

We must know the depth of the problem; otherwise, we will not go for the solution. When death happens, our consciousness will be torn from the body. There will be severe pain. Immediately, we will go into coma. Doctors say that coma is an automatic mechanism to combat the pain. It is automatic anaesthesia. That is why, every ordinary men fall into coma before they leave the body. Only enlightened masters have conscious deaths. There is no need for them to go into a coma. Many enlightened masters have passed away in the sitting posture. Paramahamsa Yogananda was one of them.

Next, in the *pranic* space, our desires want to possess our body, but time refuses to allow them to do so. It is time to leave and move to the next body. In the struggle between our desires and time, it is time that wins. Like this, step by step we move into different spaces and enter the next body. We enter into another body in 3 *kshanas* (*kshana* is defined as the time between two thoughts).

As long as we are in this body, we see the whole world in four dimensions. We have seen movies in three dimensions where we feel that we are a part of the scene. But in 4D movies, they also make us experience it by rocking our chairs and causing some special effects at the physical level! For example, if we are sitting and there is an earthquake being shown, we will not just be watching it but we will also experience it! When we are in this body, the outer world is exciting and colourful; meditation and spirituality take the back-seat. They don't seem important or necessary. We feel that these can wait. But the moment we leave the body and start travelling inside, the outwardly trip becomes inconsequential and meditation and other spiritual interests become more important and enjoyable. As long as we are in this physical body, we continuously chase material things to make our lives comfortable.

People come and tell me that they don't have time for meditation. I tell them to take back their words. Be honest and accept that you don't have the interest. At least be clear to yourself that your priority is not meditation. Our aim is to make more money, and make our life comfortable. Be honest to yourself about it. Our money and status, our social life, will not contribute to anything when we leave the body. Remember that.

~ Live with Consciousness Rather Than with Conscience

All the things that we have lived for have no place in the zone that we experience as we leave our body. Our sins and good deeds bear no value. There are no bargains for us to have. Our charitable donations have no say there. There can be no money exchange. We cannot give donations to a charitable institution and take the receipt along with us. There is no visa or speed-pass in heaven. There is no exchange counter between earth and heaven.

A small story:

One man managed to strike a conversation with God. He spoke to him about heaven and hell.
God said to him, 'Come, I will show you hell.'
They entered a room where a group of people sat around a huge pot of stew. Everyone was looking famished.
Each held a spoon that reached the pot, but the spoon had a handle so much longer than their arms that it could not be used to get the stew into their own mouths. The suffering was terrible.
God said after a while, 'Come, now I will show you heaven.'
They entered another room, identical to the first - the pot of stew, the group of people, the same long-handled spoons. But there everyone was happy and well-nourished.
'I don't understand,' said the man. 'Why are they happy here when they were miserable in the other room and everything was the same?'
God smiled and said, 'It is simple. Here they have learnt to feed each other!'

Geographically, there is no hell or heaven. These are only psychological states. How much we learn to go with the flow and live, that much life can be heaven. If we are intelligent, we will be happy and blissful; we are in heaven. Else we will remain depressed; we are in hell.

Another story:

A big industrialist died and reached the office of St. Peter.
St. Peter gave him a choice to be in heaven or in hell.
The industrialist requested to be taken to both the places before he could decide.

The request was granted. First, he went to heaven. There he saw only saints singing hymns. There was no great activity.
Next he went to hell where he saw people dancing and drinking and having fun. There was a celebration going on. The industrialist was very impressed and decided to choose hell.
St. Peter agreed but warned him that once the decision was made there was no going back.
The industrialist was confident of his decision and went ahead with his choice of hell.
The industrialist was taken to hell. The moment he stepped into hell, he was grabbed by two devils who started torturing him. He was very upset. He protested and blamed the authorities for this treatment. He said, 'This is not what I saw when I came to inspect! It was so lively and inviting. Now what I see is completely different. I feel cheated now!'
The demons looked at him and replied, 'What you saw was only our marketing department!'

Understand that if we believe in heaven and hell, we will end up only in the marketing department! All our ideas of merits and sins are created for better social life. They are not spiritual laws. Only consciousness can help us; not our conscience. Our consciousness is natural; it is a continuous witnessing awareness. Only that is going to guide us after death.

Going to temples and places of worship is not going to help us after death. If we think that leading a religious life here is going to help us there, be very clear that you are not going to be rewarded there. Our actions are not going to accompany us. The moment we leave this physical layer, our activities are not going to count. Whether we are sinners or saints does not count either. There is no difference between a *sadhu* (one who has renounced family life) and a householder; this is only a social difference. At the time of leaving the body, what matters is how the person has lived; how aware he has been.

How consciously we have lived life is all that counts. The more we become aware of our body and mind, the more it comes under our control. Someone once asked me, 'By controlling my desire for sex, can I attain enlightenment?' I told him, if you are enlightened, you will not have the desire for sex. But don't think that by controlling your desire for sex, you will become enlightened. We must understand that an enlightened man is out of the sex circle. Buddha was out of sex, Krishna was out of sex and Jesus was out of sex.

A small story from Krishna's life:

Once, Krishna along with the gopis (cowherd devotees of Krishna), was trying to cross the sacred river Yamuna (river in northern India) which was heavily flooded at that time.
He prayed to Yamuna to subside and give Him way if she believed He was a brahmachari (celibate).
Yamuna subsided at once to give them way.
People wondered how this was possible since to them, Krishna was a flirt! He used to spend time with all His female devotees and He had thousands of wives as well. How could He be a brahmachari?
Vyasa (author of the epic - Mahabharata) explains that an enlightened master is beyond sex. He has no gender. He is beyond his body. He is beyond sex.

But an ordinary person will not attain enlightenment just by going beyond sex. It cannot be used as a technique for enlightenment. Enlightenment does not happen by suppressing ourselves. It needs transformation - of base energies to higher level energies; lust should transform to love, anger to compassion and so on. We need to work on transforming ourselves. None of our virtues or acts are going to help us after we leave the body.

A small story:

In a village, one man was charged of committing a sin. He was rounded up in the village meeting for punishment.
A wise old man visiting the village was watching the scene.
People accused the man of sin. There were shouts from all around.
The wise old man spoke loudly, 'Let the man who is without a sin pass the final judgement.'
All of a sudden, there was pin drop silence!

We are saints as long as people worship us. A 'sinner' is just an idea given to us by our enemies. A 'saint' is an idea given to us by our disciples. A sinner and saint are titles given by moralists. Ofcourse, to live in the planet, we need to follow some morality. But neither a sinner nor a saint exists once we leave the physical body. How consciously we lived our lives is the only thing that matters. Our consciousness will be the torch that will help us cross all the seven layers. Once we cross these seven layers consciously with awareness, in a meditative way, we will have the choice to be enlightened or to take birth. If we have not lived with consciousness or awareness, we will immediately enter a new body after our death. Our lust for the body will be so much that we will not even wait to get a suitable body; we will get into the first available body.

When we are living with the body, if we can be at ease with our body, if we can live with ourselves, sit without thoughts, that is what is the power of consciousness If we have the capacity to sit by ourselves without thoughts, we have the power of consciousness in us.

This is actually a very powerful Zen meditation technique: sitting with yourself. We may think that sitting without doing anything is quite easy. But if we just sit we will see how our mind races through so many thoughts, one after the other, and we will also see that most of these are disconnected and have no real reason to arise as they do! When we are with ourselves, if we are aware of thoughts as they rise, we can drop them instead of trying in vain to control them.

We can sit with everyone, but we cannot sit with ourselves. Even when we are alone, we keep ourselves busy by watching television or reading the newspaper. We watch the same things again and again; we read the same things again and again. If we are not doing these two things, we start planning or thinking.

If we can sit at least for a minute completely relaxed, we will have the same sense of relaxation when we leave the body. We will have the patience and awareness to wait and choose the right type of body. We must understand that it is we who program and design our birth, including the choice of our parents. Our choice of the next body is based on the way we have lived our lives.

For example, if we live to eat rather than eat to live, at the time of death we will still have the desire to continue eating. So we will design our next body to accommodate this desire. We will naturally choose the body of a pig! If we have lived our life only for sleeping and doing no creative work, we will choose the body of a buffalo. Based on the attitude we have lived with, we choose the next body. This is the basic idea on which our *janma-marana chakra* (cycle of life and death) revolves. We go into *janma samskara chakra,* a birth life cycle. We go and come back again taking a new body. This phenomenon happens again and again. This is the cycle of birth and death. I have given you my understanding of this cycle of birth and death from my own experience.

This is a vast subject. Only by questioning can we have a clear understanding of this subject.

Apart from the first two layers, which I have explained briefly, the third layer is the subtle layer. It is related to our guilt. When we leave this layer, there will be struggle between us and our guilt; the question of right or wrong will arise. When we leave the physical body or the *sthula sarira,* we have to deal with pain. In the *pranic* layer, we deal with desires and in the subtle layer, we deal with our guilt. The fourth body, the causal body is that of total darkness. In the fifth body which is the spiritual body, we will remember all our pain intensely. In the sixth body, the cosmic body, we will feel intense pleasure. These are the 2 spaces that I call heaven and hell. When we reach the cosmic body, we become one with consciousness. If we are not ready for it or we are not enlightened, we come back; we take a rebirth. If we are mature as we go through these layers, we become enlightened.

Even ordinary people who are not enlightened, just by their simplicity and innocence, are able to predict their death. This is very common among villagers. Even among the very family members of these people, such predictions of the person's death have been made and have come true as well. They predict the exact time!

Understand that there is nothing wrong in enjoying life. One morning, a devotee asked me about pornography. According to me, pornography is the most insensitive thing. It makes us lose sensitivity.

In this, only the body structure is respected and not the person or the being. We never feel fulfilled because it makes us insensitive. That is the reason we run behind it again and again. If we enjoyed it with our sensitivity, we would be fulfilled. I call the body, the temple of consciousness. If we enjoy it in the ultimate sense, we will get enlightened and never come back.

When we discuss enjoyment, we should see whether we are talking from a sensitive or insensitive point of view. If we are talking from an insensitive angle, we will never get enlightened. We will come back again and again. We will be stuck in the second layer. If we want to enjoy life on planet Earth, we are attracted by this desire, and we will naturally take rebirth. It is our choice whether we want to get enlightened or whether we want to enjoy the pleasures of this life on a purey materialistic plane. If our sensitivity is heightened, we enjoy bliss and are relaxed without the help of outward pleasures.

There is a beautiful *sutra* in the *Kamasutra* which says, 'The moment we have sensitivity, we realize the ecstasy and joy of living. Our very living inside our body is ecstasy.' *Tantra* calls it, 'the inner orgasm'. If we experience this, we will decide not to take another birth. Why go through all the pain of birth and death? If we have the maturity to live without the body, we will not look for another birth. But if we have any hangover, unfulfilled desire, naturally we will choose to be born again to fulfill it.

~ Live with Understanding Rather Than with Rules

The *karma* theory (theory of cause and effect) according to me has no basis. It is only a faith, a belief created by man. By creating this law, man has done a great service to society, but he has created a great conspiracy against humanity. For social well-being, this theory or law is good. For example, one implication of this law is that you will not kill me and therefore I should not kill you. It is only an understanding between people so that they can live in peace and harmony. There is no spiritual attribute to this law. But we can start giving spiritual explanation saying that we will be punished for our sins. This sense of torture is not correct. It is used to instill fear in us, so that we follow the dictum of morality as dictated by society.

When we are teaching children about morality, we could resort to telling them stories to teach them the idea of right and wrong and what repercussions can happen if they don't follow morality. But this type of fear is not necessary to make mature people understand morality.

The truth is that we carry neither our sins nor our merits with us. But we cannot say that we can do whatever we want in our lives without regard to others. What we carry with us is the mental setup. For example, a murderer carries a mindset which tortures him. Be clear, it is not the burden of a hundred murders that he actually carries with him. It is the sense of sin that he carries with him.

We think that we will go to hell if we sin. Actually it is the other way around: we sin because we *are* in hell! When we are in bliss, we cannot harm any one. It is only our conscious attitude that will make us joyful.

As long as the *karma* theory is based on fear, it will never give fulfillment. No morality should be based on fear or greed. It should be based only on understanding. Man should be given techniques to create deep awareness within him; he should be taken to an appropriate level of maturity to understand the laws. There should be no fear of hell and heaven. Surely there is no hell or heaven based on the theory of *karma*. In fact if we associate ourselves too much with so-called wrong actions, we get tied so closely to our body that we cannot disconnect ourselves from it at the time of death. This is the truth.

For instance a man who has lived only for sensual pleasures cannot leave his body easily at the time of his death. There is too much pain, and that is really what hell is.

If we live with awareness and consciousness, we will radiate joy, bliss and compassion. We will experience life to be so enjoyable and radiant, that living leaves little time for anything else.

This is the reason I never give rules even during our meditation camps. I never ask people to refrain from eating non-vegetarian food. Surprisingly, even confirmed non-vegetarians have become vegetarian after attending the meditation camps. The awareness and consciousness becomes so sharp and heightened that our very being starts guiding us. There is no need for any law. If I force vegetarianism on people, they will come up with excuses for not giving up non-vegetarian food.

So I don't believe in morality since I know it is not going to work. I believe in experience. I don't believe in conscience; I believe in consciousness. When consciousness happens in us, automatically awareness will happen in us. Social morality will start manifesting within us. There will be no conflict between inside and outside. Morality will become our life. The moment we start living rules and regulations based on morality, we will not adhere to them. It is man's basic instinct to break rules. For example, the moment we see there is no policeman or the traffic signal is not working, we start speeding. The moment we see a policeman we reduce the speed.

We try to inject the *karma* theory in a subtle way through these social laws. As long as morality is taught with fear as the basis, when morality is instilled in us from the outside, it is a result of social laws. When it is programmed inside us in our mind right from a young age, we call it the theory of *karma*. But both of these are just programming. According to me, conscience is a poor substitute to consciousness. The *karma* theory is a very poor substitute for meditation. I always tell people it is time for us to drop our toys and become mature.

A small story:

A young girl who had not seen her parents for nearly five years came home unexpectedly one day.
No sooner did she set foot inside the house than her father screamed angrily at her, 'Where have you been all this time? Look at the state you are in. You are wearing lipstick. That skirt barely covers your

legs. You left us without a word and we have not had any communication from you in five years. Why didn't you call? Do you have any idea what you've put your poor mother through?'
The girl started crying and said, 'I got into bad company. I took drugs. I became a prostitute...'
The father shouted in disbelief, 'What did you say? You are a sinner! You are a disgrace to this family. I don't ever want to see your face again!
The girl continued, 'I only came back to give mum this fur coat that I bought for her, the title deeds to a new house that I bought and a savings account certificate for one million dollars.
Her father interrupted and asked, 'What was it you said you had become again?'
The girl started crying again and said, 'A prostitute.'
The father embraced her and said, 'You scared me half to death! I thought you said 'a Protestant'!

All our morality is just skin-deep. If we look deeply, we will realize that the *karma* theory is only a societal program. People who are not programmed with *karma* theory are also alive. Social laws are social toys and *karma* theory is a mental toy.

Enough! Drop your toys and go beyond your fear and greed. Why should you do good acts just for a place in heaven? Do good acts for joy of doing it. Then the very act will bring you so much joy.

Francis Bacon says beautifully, 'Men fear death as children fear to go forth in the dark; and as that natural fear in children is increased by tales, so is the other.'

Once, one of my devotees who was handling the entire collection of money from my classes in the USA lost all the money while in the process of transferring it to the bank. Some of my very close devotees were very upset when they heard about it. I was very relaxed and calm. I told them to relax. When we are handling such big amounts, it is bound to happen. I am not worried about it. Sometimes these things happen. They were not ready to accept any explanation. They felt terribly sad because according to them, it was hard-earned money and

I had worked very hard for it. I consoled them saying that when we work intensely, the work itself is the reward and not the effect. As long as we work on the basis of greed, there will be no joy. Likewise, service should never be based on some reward.

~ DROP FEAR AND GREED

Krishna beautifully emphasizes this point in the Bhagavad Gita. When Arjuna is hesitant to fight against his cousins and relatives, Krishna tells him, 'You are a warrior; you are fighting a battle. Do your job and don't worry about the fruits of your actions.'

There is need to worry about fear and greed; no need to fear about punishment and reward. If we are only living our lives based on fear and greed, be sure that we are not mature. We have aged, but not grown up. All these theories about *karma* are good to start with, but not to end at.

Someone asked Vivekananda, 'What is the need to believe in the Bible? Should I actually believe in heaven and hell?' Vivekananda replied, 'It is good to be born in the church, but not to die there.'

It is good to start with a little bit of force and fear. To start with, when fear is used to make children understand, it is okay. They may need it for understanding certain concepts. But adults have no need for it. We should be mature enough to understand.

Vivekananda said, 'Flood your spirituality and religion with logic and reasoning. Whatever withstands these, let it stay; let the others be washed away. The sooner it is washed away, the better it is for mankind.' We have had enough of living with *Manusmruti* (ancient Indian religious text for moral living). Of course, Manu had done a great service to mankind by laying down guidelines for social interaction, but we have to go beyond *Smruti,* the laws that were laid down to reach *Sruti,* the divine truths.

There are two types of scriptures in Eastern mysticism - one is *Smruti*: day-to-day laws such as social laws laid down as religious truths and regulations, and the other is *Sruti*: inner spiritual qualities to improve one's consciousness that the great sages internalized as they contemplated infinite cosmic power. The *Upanishads* constitute *Sruti*, while the *Puranas*, including *Manusmruti*, constitute the *Smrutis*.

Hindu religion was originally called *Sanatana Dharma*, the eternal way of righteous living. *Sanatana Dharma* is the only religious philosophy which has the courage to say that *Smrutis*, religious laws can be changed. It declares that its scriptures can be updated. It says that its students have the right to do so. *Rishis* (sages) say that when the *Smrutis* are changed, the entire society can be changed. *Sruti* is the technique to consciousness.

The desires and thoughts which we have in this birth if fulfilled can lead to either of two things: deep satisfaction and fulfillment or unfulfillment and hopelessness. If we have led a complete life and satisfied all our desires, there is no need to come back. But if we have not lived our desires, we will come back again to fulfill the unfulfilled desires. To fulfill these desires, we will choose our parents, birth-place and friends. We will carry with us the same mental setup and tendency to do the same kind of things.

For example, if we cheat somebody in this life, in the next life we may not be cheated by that same person but we will carry the same attitude of cheating with us and whatever we gain by cheating, we will never enjoy. We will not have the sensitivity to enjoy it. We will be in deep dissatisfaction. This is like having an expensive bed to sleep on but lacking the ability to sleep!

By carrying the same mental setup, we will hurt others as well as ourselves.

Someone once asked me what the difference was between awareness and consciousness. Awareness is the starting point and consciousness is the end, the state of enlightenment. The process starts with awareness, and ends with consciousness. Awareness is like 18 carat gold, while consciousness is like 24 carat gold!

A beautiful real-life story from the life of Viktor Frankl, author of the inspiring book, 'Man's Search for Meaning'.

Frankl was a Jew, a practicing psychiatrist who lived in the days of Nazi Germany.
He along with his entire family, were sent to a concentration camp by the Nazis. His family, except for his sister, perished in the Holocaust. Frankl suffered a lot of indignity and torture and lived life by the moment, never knowing what the next moment had in store for him - whether it was the gas chamber for himself, or whether he would have to shovel out the bodies of his fellow inmates.
One day, when he was alone in his room, he suddenly became aware of what he calls, 'the last of the human freedoms'. He realized that his captors could control the entire external environment, but one thing they could never control, was his actual self, his choice of how to handle himself and his reactions to what happened in his life.
He realized at that instant, that even though things happened in his external world out of his control, his response to it was still in his hands; it was ultimately his choice. It was up to him to choose whether he got frustrated and depressed or whether he could look at the events as an unaffected observer, aware of his true identity. This gave him tremendous strength which radiated to the others as well who were facing this unimaginable torture and helped them find meaning and dignity in their existence.

This is what led him to declare ultimately: man should not ask what the meaning of his life was, but rather must recognize that it is he who is asked. Each man is questioned by life and he can only answer to his own life; to life, he can only respond by being responsible.

Consciousness is pure energy and intelligence. We attribute many things to it. No attribute can actually describe it completely because no attribute exists in it. It is devoid of any attributes. It is our innermost self. Sankara talks beautifully about consciousness. He says in a Sanskrit *sloka*, 'Even if we do *abisheka* (offering) and rituals for one *yuga* (tens of thousands of years), it is not going to help unless we understand consciousness.'

Devotion helps but devotional activities which are the outwardly activities like pouring milk or water on the deity, done without awareness are not going to help. If we feel that God is residing in us and we can relate to Him deeply, it is going to definitely help. Physical activities are not going to help. Working in the line of awareness and working for improving one's consciousness through meditation is the only solution.

I speak the truth bluntly; this does hurt some people. They run away from me. When I ask people to drop something, they drop me! The master is like a rotating diamond; he cuts through and exposes the diamond in us. The truth will transform all the lies in our life that we are carrying. But just like how a diamond cuts, this uncovering of the truth cuts and this hurts our ego.

Your seeing me is a dream. The scriptures say: the moment we **see** an enlightened master, we become enlightened.

Seeing me is not the same as looking at me, which is what you do. Looking is with the eyes, seeing is with the being. The closer you come to the master, the more your understanding of him changes. Your maturity allows you to see me differently.

When I speak the truth, you are not ready to listen, since you are caught up in their outer world. You feel cozy and comfortable in it. After all, truths are hard to digest. You want to escape them. You fool yourselves by thinking that the life you are leading is fine. Little do you realize that at the time of leaving the body, you are going to undergo unimaginable pain. At that time, you will feel that you missed out on me. You will have an intense guilt for not listening to me. This experience of pain and guilt will make you decide not to miss me in your next birth. Unfortunately, at the time of delivery, you go into voluntary coma because of the intense pain. You lose the past memory. The past is wiped out from memory. Again, in this life, we may meet an updated version of Paramahamsa Nithyananda but we miss Him once again.

Only at the time of departing from the body, we realize our mistake; we get our consciousness back. Our memory comes back. Then, we take a rebirth. Some people, after missing this consciousness two or three times during their life-time, decide not to miss it again at any cost. Many of them decide to go to the extent of coming back with some disease. They feel that at least the disease will be a constant reminder that will ensure they do not miss Him. Some of my inner circle devotees who have come to me had cancer and other major diseases; they have been cured. They decided to stay on with me.

A devotee once told me, 'Master, my cancer was my own creation. Otherwise, I wouldn't have come to you.' People bring the diseases with them, so that they can be with the Master, even if their ego gets hurt.

~ THERE IS A BEAUTIFUL STORY FROM TAMIL LITERATURE:

A great poet, Appar, missed his spiritual path and the possibility of enlightenment in two or three births. The next time, when he took birth, he came with a stomach problem. He says the stomach problem was to be a constant reminder to his enlightenment. He came with the attitude, 'Let me suffer with this stomach problem till I get enlightened.' The moment he got enlightened, the stomach problem left him.

In the *Mahabharata*, Kunti, mother of the five Pandava princes, prays to Krishna, 'Let pain and sufferings come from the four corners of the world. This will make me constantly remember you, O Krishna! This will constantly remind me of my goal, my only goal of enlightenment.' This is a technique for enlightenment. Some people even bring depression.

Take the example of Lance Armstrong, the famous biker who has become the epitome of courage and grit.

Lance was a very successful professional biker who was ranked number one in the world. He won a number of prestigious tournaments and was at the top of his career when he was literally forced off his bike by an excruciating pain. To his horror, he was diagnosed with cancer that had spread all over his body. But his courage and determination made him not just work towards getting back to normal but also gave him the strength to get back to his passion for biking. He totally recovered from the deadly disease. But it had taught him to look at life with a broader perspective and he wanted to work towards awareness of cancer and help the thousands of people who are going through what he underwent. He trained hard enough and returned to not just participate but to win the most strenuous cycling championships - Tour de France - 6 times! What to most people would have come as a lethal blow, killing the spirit and eventually the body, became a turning point for this man, who has now become a great source of inspiration and hope for thousands of people.

However, there is absolutely no need to take a few births, then come back with some serious disease in order to get enlightened. In this *janma* (birth), you can do it. Don't miss it! Just use your intelligence.

~ ONLY INCIDENTS, NO ACCIDENTS

In three *kshanas*, we enter a new body when we are reborn. There is a hangover for thirteen days. For thirteen days, children will not have individual consciousness; they will not have total awareness. For thirteen days, the transfer of mental setup happens. The *shraddha* ceremony for the dead (last rites in Eastern custom) helps the *jiva* (soul) to leave the body easily and enter another body. During *shraddha*, the *Katopanishad* is read. It is said that all the truths are chanted in the form of *mantras*. It helps the *jiva* be relaxed and go into *atma jnana*, self-awareness or enlightenment. These *mantras* give the right knowledge to the *jiva*. This is to enable the *jiva* to realize these truths in the next birth.

When we come back, we come with certain ideas of what we want to achieve, how to live and how much strength we want to have for the body. Once the body has run enough, unconsciousness settles in. Our body starts feeling tired progressively and one fine day we leave it.

Accidents are also in a way unconsciously invited by us. Logically, we can't understand how we can invite accidents. When we choose more comfort, better life, we invite risks also. When we have deep fear in our minds, it can invite accidents. Just like the antenna attracts the satellite waves, our mental setup attracts incidents in our lives towards us.

Some one asked me why anybody would want to be born in a beggar family out of choice.

It is the conscious choice of that being. Wealth brings comfort and responsibility too. The being would have had enough of responsibility and therefore chosen the apparent suffering of a beggar family.

> *I was once called to heal an autistic child in America. As I touched him, his being talked to me in Tamil though nobody in the family knew Tamil. He said to me rudely, 'Take away your hand! I do not want your healing!' I asked the being, 'Who are you?' He said, 'Don't bother me; it is none of your business! I do not want any responsibility in this life and I am very happy as an autistic person.' I asked him, 'Why did you choose these nice people as your parents? Why are you torturing them? They are not happy because of you, though you may be happy.' He said, 'They are good people and that is why I came to them. Since they are good people, I knew they would take care of me.'*

If we are blissful, people with similar attitudes will be attracted towards us. If we are dull, lethargic and depressed, the same type of people will be attracted towards us. We will fall in line with the people who have the same mental setup. We attract incidents based on our mental setup.

If a person has taken birth with the intention of living a hundred years, but commits suicide before that, for the remaining years of his destined life, he will be without a body. This is what we call ghosts. In the case of accidents, if the person has had a glimpse of meditation, or lived consciously till until the accident, the person will be given the next body immediately. If before the accident, he has lived unconsciously and has not had a glimpse of meditation, he has to wait for his body just like people who have committed suicide. The suffering in those remaining years is great. They will feel the whole world but they cannot enjoy it. It is like placing a variety of sweets before a man who cannot use his hands to reach the sweets!

Suicide is the worst crime. These people who are without a body try to take over the bodies of people with low awareness and try to possess them. This is what happens when a person is possessed by a ghost. A meditator can never be possessed or troubled by a ghost because his awareness and consciousness is high.

So never postpone meditation, since accidents cannot be predicted!

In this life, meditation will help the whole family because the house will be filled with positive energy and vibrations. Our well-being and joyous mood will be felt by other family members and they will also benefit. At the time of death, meditation will help only you and not the others in your family.

Krishna says, 'Whatever we choose at the moment of death, that will become our reality in the next birth; we will be that.' Some people think that they can manage, if they remind themselves to think of the Almighty, the divine Existence in the last moment of their lives. That will never happen unless we make that a habit all our lives. If we repeat the words 'Coca-Cola' our entire lives, we cannot and will not think of Rama or Krishna in our last moment!

Many argue with me about what Krishna says about *karma* in the *Bhagavad Gita*. They say that an entire chapter of the *Gita* is devoted only to the explanation of the *karma* theory: what we do in this life not only affects us in this life, but also in future lives; similarly, what we have done in past lives will influence what happens to us in this life. All this is correct factually.

Krishna plays multiple roles in our lives. He is our teacher in our primary and middle school and professor in our college and university education. He teaches us step-by-step. He is a teacher at every level. So when He talks about the theory of *karma*, it is only for learning at the initial level. He prepares us for greater understanding. He talks about our last desire becoming our desired reality in our next birth. It takes great awareness to understand the words of an enlightened master such as Krishna.

During the wonderful exposition of the *Bhagavad Gita* by Krishna, after hearing about the different types of yoga, Arjuna confesses to Krishna, 'Oh, Krishna! You have confused me totally. I was better off before I spoke to you. Now, I am utterly confused. What should I do?' Krishna replies, 'That is exactly what I wanted to happen. Drop all your so called *dharma*, moral and righteous living, societal conditioning, your value systems, beliefs and understandings. Surrender to me.' Here, surrender refers not to the form of Krishna, but to His energy: the cosmic intelligence, *Parashakti*. He says, 'Surrender to me and I will liberate you from everything.'

Krishna is teaching Arjuna step by step. You may ask me, how can we object to Krishna by saying that the *karma* theory is wrong? You see: I am not the one who is objecting. Krishna Himself is objecting to the *karma* theory and rewriting it as he continues to teach Arjuna in the *Gita*. He waits for Arjuna's awareness to grow so that he can progress from the gross facts of living to its subtler truths.

When a person is learning to cycle, we tell him to keep his hand on the handle, sit straight and keep his feet on the pedals. The moment he learns it though, he starts doing stunts on the bicycle.

I am teaching you the Ultimate lesson: the Mystery of Mysteries.

Free will is not free will as we think. Destiny is not destiny as we think. We are here because of our past decisions. Take the example of a person who has come to my meditation camp. First, he saw the flyer announcing the details of my meditation program; then he noted down the place and decided to call the organizer. He decided to take the driving directions; then he decided to drive, arrived, sat in the hall and decided to listen. The questioning in the mediation program about various things happens because of the totality of his decisions.

Fate or destiny is the path we create. But after creating it, we forget that we created it when we face the consequences.

As the *Upanishads* put it beautifully:

We are what our deep driving desire is,
As is our desire, so is our will,
As is our will, so is our act,
As is our act, so is our Destiny.

It is we who choose something without knowing its after-effects. This is like going to a restaurant, eating whatever we want and then when we finally get the bill, we are shocked and refuse to pay the bill, saying we have only ordered the food but not the bill!

The present is a result of all our past decisions and our future will be a consequence of all our present decisions. The problem is, many of our decisions are made unconsciously. So when situations arise, we don't take responsibility for it. We have forgotten our past decisions.

We lack understanding here. All our present is only the result of our past decisions and all our future is only the effect of our present decisions. Be aware of your present; that is enough. There is no need to worry about the past or the future. By doing this, we will be able to design our future in a beautiful way. Then, there is no need to be concerned about destiny and free will.

Buddha teaches, 'Do not dwell in the past, do not dream of the future, concentrate the mind on the present moment.'

A beautiful question: the world population is increasing so much. Where are they all coming from? The answer is: of course, from the countless animals being killed everyday everywhere. These animals are coming as the increased population! No wonder so many people on this Earth today are behaving like animals!

~ Meditation - The Key to Consciousness

Having the right master and practicing meditation is essential. Even a glimpse of joy or deep feeling while meditating is enough. The NSP is a gift from me to this world. I make you work on the seven layers of the energy body during this program. You will get a glimpse of the higher consciousness at least in one layer.

Many people come and tell me about their experiences of intense joy during the LBP that is the precursor to the NSP. They say they have never experienced such joy or bliss in their lives. Even a glimpse of joy or bliss will make you understand that it is possible, even without the body. That will act as a torch or a guide throughout your life especially at the time of death. A continuous practice of meditation will be a path-finder and will definitely help you at the time of death.

One glimpse is enough to change your mental setup. It can change your entire life. So instead of asking how long one should meditate, it is better to ask how intensely one should meditate!

As Emerson, the American essayist and poet says, 'It is not the length of life, but the depth of life.'

If we have just one glimpse of consciousness and awareness and if we maintain it with a simple meditation technique, it is enough to penetrate the seven layers. If our meditation has given us a conscious experience, we don't have to remember it. At the time of death, our whole life will be relived before us. It will be just like a fast rewind. Within a few minutes, our entire life's incidents will be flashed before us. If the glimpse has been deep and intense, it will help us at this time. Its intensity will surpass the pain which we will be going through.

If we have been meditating for thirty years and still have not had even one glimpse, something is wrong. According to me, one year is too much if you are with me, to have a glimpse of consciousness.

Until we get a glimpse, we have to keep our eyes closed and do the meditation. Once you have the glimpse, there is no need to sit down, close your eyes and meditate, since every moment you will be joyous. Eating, sleeping, walking or sitting, you will be in continuous joy. With eyes open, you can see God.

~ WHAT IS PAIN AND PLEASURE?

Try this experiment: Take a green chilli in one hand and sugar in the other hand. Meditate and touch either side of our tongue with these two. There will be no difference between them. It is we who say that something is hot or cold, sweet or bitter. We are so unconscious that we keep on qualifying all our experiences as pain or pleasure.

There is no difference between suffering and joy. If we go beyond both, we experience bliss, come what may. We continuously pigeon-hole our experiences. That is the reason we see suffering as suffering and joy as joy. We judge the present moment based on our past experience. If you analyze this deeply, you will realize that you are not living in the present; you are just 're-living' the past.

A small story:

> *An elderly man was returning to his village after a few months, after attending to some work in the next village.*
> *Suddenly, he sees that his hut is on fire. He starts wailing and running around, as he cannot do anything about it.*
> *Just then, one of his sons comes running to him and says, 'Father, don't worry! We just sold our house to our neighbors yesterday.'*
> *Hearing this, the man was overjoyed that the burning house was no longer in his possession. He started dancing around.*
> *Just then, his wife comes running and anxiously tells him, 'But we have not yet received the payment for the house!'*
> *The minute the man hears this, he starts wailing again and is grief-stricken.*

Within half an hour, the man has had three different moods. The same house is burning and the same person is seeing this. Within half an hour, he has felt deep pain, deep pleasure and deep pain again!

Pain and pleasure are our rubber-stamps. It is our idea! Both pain and pleasure are part of our psycho-drama. Even without meditation if we feel the truth consciously, we will feel liberated. But when emotions start erupting unconsciously, our conscious will not be under our control. For that we need meditation. As long as we are balanced, all the logic and reasoning will work. But when we are confronted directly by these imbalances, we see a problem. If we are balanced even at that time, we are truly liberated. When we are imbalanced, only meditation will give us the power and energy to shift the balance.

If we have a glimpse of consciousness, we will have an understanding of the *samatva,* the sameness, the non-differentiation between these emotions. All our understanding of *samatva* right now is wrong. Our idea of *samatva* is based only on the dictionary meaning. After the glimpse, it will be experiential.

A small story:

> *A woman was wearing a fur coat and admiring herself in front of the mirror. She felt it looked really good on her.*
> *Her daughter looked at her and said, 'Mom, how much the poor animal must have suffered for you to get this coat!'*
> *The lady was furious and shouted at her daughter, 'How dare you speak of your father like that!'*

The little girl was talking about the furry animal that was killed in order for the coat to be made. But the mother totally misinterpreted her comment and scolded her for talking about her father who had worked to get her the coat! Her daughter's description matched the image of her husband as a man who had to work really hard to earn enough so they could afford to buy her coat.

So understand: experiential understanding is different from the dictionary meaning. Only when we have this experience, will we understand what Krishna meant by *samatva*.

Even the word 'sex' has two different meanings: the dictionary meaning and the existential meaning born out of meditation.

Buddha was intelligent: he tried thousands of meditation techniques and ultimately became enlightened. He worked with thousands of keys and ultimately found the right key. If we have the courage, we can also do it.

That is why Buddha says with authority, 'To be idle is a short road to death and to be diligent is a way of life; foolish people are idle, wise people are diligent.'

Think about it: if it were us in the place of Buddha, forget twelve years of trying, we would not have been able to do meditation for more than a couple of days! Our ego would not have allowed us to continue. We would be cheating ourselves. Buddha belonged to a different level. We may not be able to do what He did. But atleast we can learn to improve. We always aim very high. We want to fly when we are not even able to walk. Accept reality and start walking first; you will automatically fly!

Forget *vaastu* (ancient Indian science relating to house-building), gemology, astrology andnumerology; just do meditation. The experience will stand by you at the time of death. It will help you have a painless transition. Understand the truth of dying and you can start living better.

The final step in the NSP is to reach the nirvanic layer. By the time one reaches this layer, one will be without *samskaras*; one is at the doorstep of enlightenment. We have to let go to reach enlightenment. Enlightenment just happens; it cannot be made to happen. It is like river water. It stays in our hands as long as our hands are open; once we close our hands there is no water.

~ The Purposelessness of Life

Bliss is choicelessness. If we try to make bliss a choice, it will be absent. If we can understand the purposelessness of life as a part of the grand plan of Existence, we will reach this layer.

Ego believes that there is purpose to life: material, relational and spiritual. The more the purpose, the stronger our ego feels. If we drop all other purposes and still hold on to the purpose of enlightenment, it is futile. Only when we realize that life is totally purposeless and drop our ego will enlightenment happen to us.

Even if you look at it logically, what is the purpose of Existence? Could God who creates everything else, including jungles, not have created concrete jungles and cities as well? The purpose of Existence is bliss, that is all!

How can we enjoy without possessing, without making something our own? We are like water bubbles on a wave in the ocean. Each bubble catches hold of a few more bubbles labeling them as wife, husband, father and son. The bubble collects sand particles thinking they are jewels, since it does not understand that it can burst any moment!

When we are ready to digest that everything is purposeless, including material, relational and spiritual objects, only then life acquires meaning. When we have a goal we miss the path! We miss the joy of the path.

The mind waits for something to happen. It waits for salary: weekly, monthly, yearly, five-yearly. When we measure life by pay cheques, we reduce our spirit to matter.

Our ego is stuck on what we see as a purpose in life. We think that after we settle our social responsibilities, we will take up the spiritual path. An elderly lady came to me with her son. She wanted me to take him into the ashram as a *brahmachari* (young boy who stays single and follows certain vows to follow reality instead of fantasies). I was surprised since usually no parent would like their child to be a *brahmachari*. Many think that Vivekananda is great, but no one wants his own son to be a Vivekananda. They can't imagine how their child can be so blissful. I asked her to tell me why she wanted him to be at the ashram. She said that he was mentally unsound. I told her politely, '*Amma*, I run an ashram, not an asylum!'

We have many reasons why we cannot do things. We say, 'If I didn't have this responsibility, I would be with the master.' By the time we finish one responsibility, we will have ten more waiting for us! Running has become our conditioning, not relaxing. When we are young, we tell ourselves that we will relax after we graduate from university; then we shift the goal post to marriage; then to children; then to educating children; then their marriage. Can we relax after we are sixty? By then we miss the path and we forget how to relax!

The primal sin we can commit is to miss the path of life by following goals. When we live, let us allow our being to be blissful. When we start hurrying, think about what we are hurrying for. Do not allow restlessness in you hoping it will settle; that will never happen. If we are not able to relax into the present moment even after fulfilling our responsibilities, we will still feel unfulfilled. Whenever we run, when we hurry, think 'why', 'what for'?

We may have a big house, drive a big car, and people around us may be always praising us. Can we carry any of this with us into the afterlife? Can we carry even one single cheque book with us? It is all purposeless.

When we understand this purposelessness, healing happens. Even if we have been abused, we will heal. if we allow this understanding to happen, the understanding itself will guide us.

We may ask, 'What kind of teaching is this? All my life I have had a purpose, and my life has been fine. Now you say that everything is without purpose!' Whether you like it or not, this is the truth.

People are shocked when I say this.They begin to think, 'Now I know life is purposeless. I should not go to work. I should not take a vacation.' This is wrong understanding. Once we have the understanding of purposelessness, we can never be lazy. *Tamas* (laziness) cannot come out of intelligence. Perhaps for two days you will just lie in bed and not get up. The third day, you will wake up as a different person, without restlessness; restlessness is a monster that you would have conquered.

Restlessness hides purposelessness from us; it hides the path using goals. Please understand this and be healed. All our dreams of the future and all our guilt of the past will disappear; all ephemeral joys and suffering will vanish.

In Tiruvannamalai, there was an enlightened master by name Ram Surat Kumar. He was as innocent as a child. Whenever people came to him, whatever their problem was, he would say 'Alright'. When someone died, he said, 'Alright.' When someone told him, 'My son is getting married', he would say, 'Alright.' I asked him, 'Master, why do you say 'alright' to everything?' He said, 'Everything is just purposeless. Whatever we think has a purpose, has no meaning.'

Whenever we remember the truth of purposelessness, healing will happen; suffering will disappear. Whether we have something or do not have, neither will have purpose.

We need courage to pursue the truth. Then, life will take a different path. We will live as a liberated soul. We will never drop our job, relationship or wealth. We will drop only what we do not have. We will drop the mental associations. We will drop the fantasy of a throne and start enjoying the seat. When purpose is dropped, meaning will happen.

When you wake up in the morning, just laugh! If you cannot feel free to laugh in your own home, where else can you laugh? Laugh at how purposeless everything is. Release yourself from the nagging of restlessness. There is no need to sell our inner space to have outer space. We can retain the joy inside and still have outer space to enjoy.

When we have fear, we are enslaved. It is a social conditioning. Drop it! Our very quality of life will change. Once we understand freedom, we cannot be enslaved any more.

The Master is there to awaken this understanding of freedom in us. Ramana says, Guru is a *simha swapna,* a nightmare, a lion that chases you until you are fully awake! You will wake up even if you are not in a dream!

Sex, Death and Meditation

Sex, Death and Meditation - are these really contradictory?

Sex, meditation and death: when I chose this title, one of my ashram residents was sitting next to me. I was selecting titles for the discourses to be given in America. When I chose this title, she commented, 'Master, these are totally contradictory words forming a title. How can you talk about them in the same discourse?'

I gave her the explanation as to why they are all combined together. Of course, even after the explanation, when we hear the title we will feel that these are totally contradictory words.

When all three are impure, they are totally opposite to each other, contradictory to each other. When meditation starts happening in our lives, it can purify sex and death and ultimately combine all the three experiences into one. When we reach spiritual life which is the ultimate goal of any being, we will understand things differently.

We will see all these three terms in three different planes. First, we will see how in an impure state these terms are contradictory to one another; then, when we add meditation, how they start complementing each other, and finally when meditation ends, how they become one with each other.

First, let us see how these three words and experiences that they connote, contradict each other; then, how they complement each other and finally, how they become one as they meet and merge.

~ COMMON PERCEPTION OF DEATH

The basic understanding as of now that we have of death is 'fear'. There is fear and greed but I will start from fear because we understand fear more clearly than greed; fear is a layer deeper than greed. We think that from greed fear appears. No! It is the other way around: from fear, greed appears.

'I' is the root of fear; 'mine' is the root of greed. 'I' is the ego: the being and the root of fear; 'mine' is the sense of possession. We say, 'this is mine, that is mine, this is my house, this is my car, this is my bungalow, these are my relations, these are my friends.' 'Mine' is the root of greed. 'I' is the root of fear. That is why the loss of the ego, the loss of 'I' seems so traumatic, so fearful.

So let me explain about death. The minute we hear the word death, what happens to us? The very word creates agony; the very word creates fear. The very word! Immediately we think: why should we talk about all this now? We will handle it when it arrives. Why should we think about this now? There is a deep fear in us where we think that just the very thinking will invite death to our homes!

In most cultures, death is not discussed openly. Youngsters are discouraged from talking about it. It is considered inauspicious. If there is any death in the family, the children are kept away. They are not allowed to be around for the funeral. I don't know whether it happens in this culture as well. Any kind of loss is pushed under a mental carpet!

Something that is so natural, so normal in the larger cycle of life is turned into an abnormal, fearful thing.

Therefore from a very young age, we build an impression of death as a fearful enemy that must be kept at an arm's length. On the one hand, we long for happiness and freedom. On the other hand, we fear of letting go of all our alleged securities. This makes us build so many walls that we finally end up entombing ourselves.

If you are in a room and you know you have the keys to the room, you know that you are free to stay in the room as long as possible and leave it when you want to. However, if you do not know about the keys to the room, even when you are in the room willingly, you will always be afraid of being locked up with no means of going out. This is exactly what happens with us when we think that we need to escape from death, but do not know how to, and at the same time want to enjoy the freedom of life.

Please understand that unless we throw ourselves into the utter insecurity of Existence, we will never experience real freedom, real bliss.

As of now, our understanding about death is totally negative. Death is seen as an enemy. That is why, in all religions, in all cultures, death is painted as black. In Hinduism, Yama is black; in Christianity, Satan is black; in Buddhism, Mara is black. In all religions, death is painted in black. We paint death like a villain, never like a hero; death is always painted as a villain. The idea of death is always approached with negativity; we feel death takes away everything from us. Whatever we want, whatever we enjoy, whatever we have, is just snatched by force from us. We always want to escape death.

~ THE STRUGGLE AGAINST THE SINGLE CERTAINTY OF LIFE-DEATH

From time immemorial, all traditions, all civilizations have been trying all possible ways to conquer death. Scientists try through medicines, which is responsible for the birth and growth of allopathy.

Siddhas, the *ayurvaidyas* (traditional Hindu doctors), tried through herbs, which gave birth to the *siddha* tradition and *kayakalpa* (anti-ageing medicine). The *yogis* tried through *mantras*, which gave birth to the *mrutyunjaya mantra* (chat to overcome fear of death) and *pranayama* (breath control) techniques. The Lamas tried through meditation, which gave birth to our *Mahamantra* meditation technique to energize the heart energy centre, *anahata chakra*. Almost all traditions, all cultures have tried to conquer death, to go beyond death. Why?

Why is all of humanity struggling against the one thing and that too, the only thing that is a certainty in all our lives? Can we make the whole earth flat? No! It is a proven fact that the earth is round. But if we struggle against this fact, then there is something wrong in our struggle, in our understanding. It is the same with death too. Why are we struggling to accept the truth when even after such a lot of struggle, not a single human being has been successful in mastering or overcoming death.

There was this person in Tamil Nadu, India, who claimed to be a great spiritual figure. In India, one needs nothing more than a few pamphlets to proclaim that one is a spiritual teacher! In other religions, one would need to get the agreement of the headquarters or the organizational president. In Hinduism, we don't need anything: just a small amount of money to print pamphlets is more than enough.

This man claimed that in the year 2000, the whole world would be destroyed. He predicted that he would be the sole human being who would survive the *pralaya* (final dissolution). Being a good orator, he convinced thousands of people about the impending doomsday through mass meetings and popular media. He claimed that if they aligned with his preaching, they would be saved from this horrible fate that was sure to be theirs otherwise. What happened finally? One fine day, the papers carried the news that he had died! Instead of the world dying, he was dead!

What did this man do? He played with the emotions of people. He tried to exploit fear in people. He capitalized on their fear that was born out of ignorance. Almost every tradition, every religion and every science, be it *allopathy, pranic healing, reiki, homeopathy, siddha,* or *ayurveda,* have worked extensively on prolonging life. Why? Why are we so anti-death? Why are we so against death? It is because we have not understood the truth or the fact behind death. We have never given ourselves the time to look into it.

Our entire society lives in denial of this one glaring truth: that dying is as much a part of our lives as living! It is this deep fear, this painful insecurity, this constant denial that is responsible for the mushrooming of so many insurance companies all over the world! How can we plan for the next fifty years when we may not be around the next fifty seconds? I tell you, life insurance is not life insurance as we are led to believe. It is actually death insurance! It is insurance for others, so many of whom may actually be waiting for us to die!

A small joke:

> *Once, a family of three went to spend an evening on the beach; a couple with their child. The man went ahead into the waves and started walking further, enjoying the water rising and falling over his feet. After some time, the child started going towards the waves as well. The mother yelled out, 'Don't go into the waves! It is dangerous, you may be swept away!' The child was surprised that his mother was shouting at him. He asked his mother, 'Why don't you allow me to go into the water? Dad is going in!' His mother replied, 'Your dad has insurance!'*

~ THE TRANSIENCE OF LIFE

Instead of teaching us to live each moment completely, joyfully, without regrets, we are trained to run our life with the energy of fear. We are trained to postpone our experiencing of life in all its variety and beauty.

Every aspect of our lives, be it concerning material objects or relationships, comes with the need for security. We start possessing things and people. We believe that material things and people give us security. What happens if there is an earthquake and all our possessions, our house, cars, money and all our savings are destroyed? Where are our objects of security? What happens if there is an accident and we lose all our loved ones? Who will we turn to? We are terrified of loss and yet, we live our whole life clinging to impermanence.

We are all like small waves in the ocean of life. As long as the wave realizes that it is an integral part of the ocean, it can be a blissful part of the grand ocean. The problem is that each wave starts thinking of itself as separate from the ocean. Not only that, it also starts thinking of the ocean as its enemy. It then starts fighting with the ocean to maintain its so-called identity. The wave starts catching other waves and labeling them saying, 'You are my parents, you are my wife, and you are my son.' It then tries to protect itself and these waves from the ocean, little realizing that all the waves are created from the same ocean; that they exist in it, and finally will fall into the same ocean!

We invest all our trust and faith in perishables. Our ignorance of death blinds us to the one truth: that the only constant thing in life is change and death is the greatest change of them all. Please understand that change is growth, and growth is life. If we start seeing death as change, then it stands to reason that it is growth, and therefore life! So what is there to be afraid of?

~ The Fear of Death is Worse than Death Itself

Once we decide that somebody is our enemy, we never look into his eyes. Whatever he does, we decide that he is doing so to agitate us. Even if he sits and has a cup of coffee or tea, we feel that he is plotting against us. Once we decide that somebody is our enemy, we don't want to have any contact with him. Similarly, once we decide that death is our enemy, we never look into it.

We are continually fighting death and in the end we just drop dead! We fight till we die. Our understanding about death, or rather our misunderstanding about death, makes death a fearful, frightening experience.

The man who resists death dies even while he lives, dies every moment because he is tortured by the very idea of death. When I say death, I don't mean only physical death. Losing anything is a form of death. Losing our comfortable life is one form of death; losing our relatives is another. Please understand that loss in any form is nothing but death.

We may ask why people are so depressed and disturbed when they lose their close relatives. Even if we are not emotionally attached to them, we are deeply affected by their death. We are more affected when we are close to them, attached to them emotionally. When our mother dies, our whole left side will suffer. When our father dies, our whole right side will suffer. The left side of the body is associated with the feminine energy while the right side is associated with the masculine energy. When our brothers die, our hands will suffer. There is a deep connection between us and our relatives. Every part of our body is connected to someone or the other.

Our being is not an individual being. It is not alone, separate, as we think. We are all interlinked. No man is an island. Everybody is interlinked. That is why we undergo terrible suffering when we lose someone or something. There is an energy loss within us. We feel empty as if we are in a void. Every 'missing' that we experience, no matter of whom or what, is what I call death.

Why are we so afraid of death? Our misunderstanding, our misconception about death makes it much more frightening than it really is. As of now, death is a totally devastating experience for us. The very word shakes us, frightens us. Nobody wants to even think about it.

~ LAUGH YOUR WAY TO LIFE NOT DEATH

If we make death a day-to-day affair, then we will never be in fear of it. People ask me surprised, 'What are you saying, Master! How is this possible?' I tell you: talk about death, crack jokes and bring it into the realm of the ordinary events of your life. Treat it like a daily chore, like going and buying your daily vegetables; make it a part and parcel of your system! Then it will lose its fearful hold over you. We will be able to laugh at ourselves; we will be able to let go.

When we laugh, we drop our seriousness. We will see that death will become our intimate friend. And contrary to our belief, death will guide us and help us to live our lives completely, from moment to moment.

A small story:

There were three Chinese mystics. Nobody knows their names now and nobody ever knew their names. They were known only as the Three Laughing Saints because they never did anything else; they simply laughed.

These three people were really beautiful: laughing with their bellies shaking. And then it would become infectious and others would start laughing. The whole marketplace would laugh.

Till just a few moments earlier, it would have been an ugly place where people were thinking only of money. Suddenly, these three mad people would come by and change the quality of the whole marketplace.

Laughter is eternal, life is eternal, the celebration always continues. The village people would forget that they had come to purchase and sell. Nobody bothered about greed. For a few seconds, a new world would open.

The saints traveled all over China, from place to place, from village to village, just helping people to laugh. Sad people, angry people, greedy people, and jealous people: they all started laughing with them. And many felt the key: we can be transformed.

In one village, it so happened that one of the three saints died. The village people gathered and they said, 'Now there will be trouble. Now we have to see how they laugh. Their friend has died; they must weep.' But when they came, the two saints were dancing, laughing and celebrating the death of their friend.

The village people said, 'Wow, this is too much! When a man is dead, it is profane to laugh and dance.' The two saints said, 'During his whole life, we laughed with him. How can we give him his last send-off with anything else? We have to laugh, we have to enjoy, we have to celebrate. This is the only way.'

The body was to be burned, and the village people said, 'We will give him a bath as the ritual prescribes.'

But the two friends said, 'Oh, our friend has said: don't perform any ritual and don't change my clothes; don't give me a bath; just put me as I am on the burning pyre.' So we have to follow his instructions.'

And then suddenly there was a great happening. When the body was put on the fire, the old man played his last trick. He had hidden many fireworks under his clothes and suddenly there was a festival of fire crackers and displays! The whole village started laughing. The two mad friends were dancing and the whole village started dancing.

It was not a death; it was a new life. Laughter is eternal, life is eternal, the celebration continues. Actors change but the drama continues. Waves change but the ocean continues. We laugh, we change and somebody else laughs but the laughter continues. We celebrate, somebody else celebrates, but the celebration continues. Existence is continuous, it is a continuum. There is not a single moment's gap in it. No death is death because every death opens a new door: it is a beginning. There is no end to life; there is always a new beginning, a resurrection.

If we change our sadness to celebration, then we will also be capable of changing our death into resurrection. So learn the art while there is still time.

~ DEATH - THE ULTIMATE AGENT OF CHANGE

All that we understand of death is that it is anti-life. Again, because of our fear, we think too much about death. The actual experience of death is not as bad as our fear of death. We project our fear and see death as a giant figure. If real death is six feet tall, because of our fear, we see it as sixty feet tall! Because of our fear, we make the six feet death look like a sixty feet tall, frightening figure!

Be very clear: no one wants to die. Even people who want to go to heaven don't want to die to get there. And yet, death is the destination we all share. No one has ever escaped it. And that is as it should be, because death is very likely the single best invention of life. It is life's change agent. It clears out the old to make way for the new. Right now the new is us, but someday, not too long from now, we will gradually become the old and be cleared away.

Our time is limited, so don't waste it living someone else's life! Don't be trapped by rigid rules, which is living with the results of other people's thinking. Don't let the noise of other's opinions drown out your own inner voice.

Most importantly, have the courage to follow your heart and intuition. Somehow, your heart already knows what you truly want to become. Everything else is secondary.

~ FANTASIES - THE ROOT OF GREED

Let us go to sex. In the same way, because of our greed, we make sex bigger than what it really is. That is why there are such huge hoardings of actors and actresses all over. All our fantasies of sex are projected outside. We contaminate true understanding of sex by creating too many imagined expectations and too many unfulfillable dreams. We in effect create the recipe for personal disaster.

A small story:

Mullah Nasruddin was bitterly complaining to one of his friends about his salary. 'I earn only twenty thousand dollars per month. I don't know how I will manage with this amount!'
His friend was surprised and asked him, 'Nasruddin, for your lifestyle, what you earn is more than enough! Why don't you feel satisfied? What was your salary when you started working?'
Nasruddin said, 'When I started, my salary was two thousand dollars. Now it is twenty thousand dollars.'
The friend was astonished, and exclaimed, 'Then why aren't you satisfied with what you have?'
Nasruddin replied, 'The moment I heard my salary was twenty thousand dollars, I began to feel I was worth one million dollars. I felt I deserved much more than what I was getting.'

Our mind projects us as someone bigger, someone greater than what we really are. The moment our existing reality changes, our imagination goes haywire! It seems like reality arrives by train while our imagination reaches by telegram. Our imagination as compared to our reality is moving on the super-fast lane. Before we can even start understanding our reality and living with it, our imagination has overtaken our life, our very existence.

In the same way, because of our ever-increasing imagination, we contaminate sex. We make our life miserable by being greedy for sex and being fearful of death. We allow both these emotions to tear us apart. This is the state that I call hell. The fabric of our whole life gets tinted with these two colors: sex and death. Both these look like the two banks of a river that will never meet and merge. We think that sex is life; death is anti-life. They seem to contradict one another.

The man who is greedy for sex is the man who is anti-death. It is deep greed that makes us want to live continuously. We want to live so that we can accumulate. The truth is that the greedier we are, the less we will enjoy what we have. Greed will drive us on to get more and more. We will never stop; we will never relax to appreciate and enjoy what is there. We are afraid that if we pause we may lose out on something.

Greed is all about the quantity of life, not the quality. We try to actualize all our sexual fantasies by getting into more and more relationships. We trap ourselves in a number game, not realizing that satisfaction depends on the depth and not the breadth of our relationships.

~ WHY RUN CONSTANTLY? LIVE IN THE MOMENT!

Sex is not confined to the possessing of another body. Nor is it about different postures. It is about the deep satisfaction that happens when two people give themselves completely: body, mind, and soul to one another. Sex is all about the sharing of our personal space in total trust with the other. It is a fearless, unconditional giving of our energy through our body and mind. It is all about being totally in the moment, in the present. It is about living with and enjoying the fullness of the reality around us.

The big problem is that we are never in the moment totally. We are afraid as to how long our joy will last and that leads us to greed for more. As a result, there is perpetual dissatisfaction.

As with death, so too with sex: it is never discussed in the open. No one wants to talk about it. Almost in all cultures, so many stories are woven around the incident of birth. Either babies are said to be brought by storks, or they are said to have been parceled by angels as gifts from God, or some kind doctor brought them home! Neither do parents discuss the topic of sex clearly with their children, nor do significant people like teachers and older relatives. In most cases, they themselves do not have the correct understanding.

If we read about sex, talk about it or discuss it, we are considered to be persons with loose morals. The natural curiosity of a child to know its own body and that of the other gender is brutally suppressed by society. The simple, beautiful truth about the process of life is never explained to young ones. People make sex shameful, secretive and yet highly desirable! This constant suppression by family and society is responsible for creating fantasies. Their whole lives revolve around working out these fantasies. They become greedy. They want the forbidden fruit. Their ignorance of the true nature of sex contaminates all their personal relationships. They see everything with tinted glasses because they don't know much about the true nature of sex; they make it bigger than what it really is!

Actually, a number of people have come and told me, 'Master, it is strange but during meditation I had an orgasmic experience! How can meditation do this?' I tell them, when we are in deep ecstasy, totally within ourselves, this can also happen. The orgasmic experience is not triggered by an external agent as we think; it is an alchemy that happens within us.

> *A dog once got a dry bone and started chewing on it. After some time, due to continuous scratching of the skin by the bone, its mouth started bleeding. The dog, thinking that the blood was coming from the bone, started relishing the bone. Little did it realize that the bone was as dry as before; it was actually relishing its own blood!*

In ancient times, during what we refer to as the *Vedic* period, there was a great system of learning called the *gurukul* (where students stayed with the guru who was an enlightened master). Here, people from a very young age were given lessons on living life effectively. The whole system addressed life in four phases: the first phase called *brahmacharya,* was a period of study that helped enhance one's aptitude, the innate potential. There was available time and guidance to explore the potentiality and allow the understanding to shape the choice of one's profession. Please understand that the word *brahmacharya* does not mean celibacy. *Brahmacharya* means living with the Truth or Reality and refers to the study of life itself.

The second phase called *grihastha,* involved adult life. This was the phase in which marriage happened. Two people, man and woman, took the sacred vow to live their life joyfully and share their energy with one another, not just their body or mind, but their whole being. Living together completely and sharing this wholeness with each other is the true essence of the *grihastha* phase.

The third phase called *vanaprastha* involved removing oneself from all forms of social struggles. When one's children were mature and ready to take on the responsibilities of their lives, one was expected to retire from active life. One had the permission from society to drop out of the rat race and take the time to grow inside. One moved into a space that would help attain a deeper understanding of oneself. The old order smoothly made way for the new.

The fourth and last phase called *sannyas* was dedicated to prepare oneself to leave planet Earth. One had lived; now it was time to pack the bags and leave. The last phase was dedicated to understanding death. One was prepared for leaving the body. Then naturally, one's life became beautiful! Living was also beautiful, leaving was also beautiful!

But now, it is an entirely different scenario. There is so much of greed within us that we want to keep on achieving something or the other until the very end. We are always running in the rat race till we drop dead. I have seen so many people who attend office till the last breath. Why? What are they trying to prove? That is nothing but another form of greed. The society that they have created feeds this greed. Such a person is admired. Such an attitude is applauded.

Understand that greed will drive us away from enjoying life. We will be so busy accumulating that we will never find the time to enjoy what we accumulate. Too much greed makes us go against the natural flow of life. It will kill us even before we can start looking at what we have accumulated!

Greed never lets us enjoy life. We are never satisfied. We keep running till running becomes our very nature. How can a man who is running all the time ever enjoy what he is running for? To do that, he needs to take time off from his constant running.

In the same way, the deep fear of death stops us from enjoying life. It makes us dull, depressed and morose. Our whole life is joyless. All the time we immerse ourselves in futile activities. We convince ourselves that the ephemeral is the real. We believe that material acquisition and relationships will give us lasting security. As a result, the fear of losing leads to the greed of hoarding. We accumulate, but we never enjoy what we have accumulated. We are not taught to let go. We are strangers to the vibrancy of life.

We are afraid to see the simple truth that is all around us: the only certainty in life is death! Life and death, sex and death, fear and greed, all these are two sides of the same coin, two banks of the same river. Right now, in the impure state, both are contradictory to one another. Once we construct the small bridge of meditation between these two banks, our whole life will be transformed!

~ Meditation - the Power to Transform our Life and Death, Greed and Fear

If we add meditation to our lives, then both sex and death get purified. We free ourselves from the clutches of sex and death, from the grip of greed and fear. The whole concept of sex and death changes completely. We grow out of both. If we really meditate, in a sense, we die and we are reborn. Our fear of death disappears; our greed for life also disappears. They are both dissolved and purified by this bridge of meditation.

Just now, we saw what death and sex are before meditation. Now let us see what they become after meditation is added to our life. We will see that the whole concept of sex, life and death changes completely. They start complementing rather than contradicting each other.

~ Death - the Ultimate Teacher

Almost all traditions have tried to conquer death, to outlive death. For some reason, all of us want to experience immortality. Only one group of really intelligent and intuitive people understood after much struggle that we were approaching death in a completely wrong manner. They decided to take a hundred and eighty degree turn. They started working with death in a different way. They used meditation as a technique to take them where others had not dared to go before. Those few intelligent ones were the *rishis* (sages) of the *Upanishad* age. The report that they submitted on their research into the phenomenon of death is called the *Katopanishad*.

Of course, I am presenting the ultimate truth. It is the truth of the struggle of the whole of humanity. It is the history of almost the whole of human consciousness. We are all familiar with the history of humanity. I am presenting the history of human consciousness. These *rishis* did research on death and finally came to the conclusion that death cannot be understood or overcome by resistance. By resisting death, we cannot go beyond death. The only way to break free of the vicious cycle of birth and death was by becoming enlightened. Entering into the death experience, penetrating death, dropping fear was the key to understanding death.

The main character of the *Katopanishad* is a small boy called Nachiketa. He meets death and faces it eye to eye, without fear. The beauty of the *Upanishad* is that for the first and last time, death is depicted as a hero. Death is portrayed as the Lord and Master, as God and *Guru*. It is God who gives all the boons and it is the Guru who gives wisdom or the ultimate intelligence. When the boy faced death squarely, without any prejudice, Yama, the Lord of Death, became the giver of material boons and the ultimate wisdom rather than the taker of life.

We may wonder, how can death give one all these things? Try to comprehend this in a different dimension, in a different way. As long as we are afraid, we will never look death in the eye. Unless and until we do that, we will never know how blessed we are with abundance. It is only when we lose something that we realize the value of that thing. Just meditate on this. Suppose you are going to die in two days, what are the things that you would want to do? How much would there be to finish? It is only when we take stock of our life that we understand how much of goodness is showered on us. We take everything for granted because we believe that we are going to live forever.

Albert Einstein says, 'There are two ways to live one's life: one is as though nothing is a miracle and the other is as though everything is a miracle!'

Only when we understand death, will we understand the preciousness of life. Once we face death without fear, we will understand that death is not the end of life but the climax. When this understanding dawns on us, we will stop praying for everlasting life.

We pray only when the question of death arises. I have seen so many atheists crying out the names of all the Gods the moment the doctor declares that they are going to die! Immediately, they turn to God for help. There are so many politicians who have come to me secretly asking for healing or for *vibhuti* (holy ash). To the world at large, they are great atheists but in their homes they worship out of sheer fear.

Then there are philosophers and the *vedantins* (followers of *Vedanta* philosophy). Just because they read a lot, they begin to think that they have become enlightened. No amount of reading can give one the experience of the written words. If we digest the food that we eat, it is transformed into energy that can be utilized in our life. If we don't digest our food properly, what happens? Our system gets disturbed and we vomit the undigested food. In the same way, if we meditate on intellectual ideas, on great philosophy, *Vedanta*, it will become our experience. If we don't meditate, we misunderstand these great truths, catch hold of people, and start vomiting on them. We will start preaching to them!

Both, our greed and our fear can be transformed by meditation. No other technique can do that which meditation can; not even prayer. Praying is just another method of escapism. Never pray out of fear. I have seen many people who start chanting the Lord's name, saying some prayer or the other, when they are walking alone on a deserted road. We remember God only when we are alone or when we are frightened. We feel good because our mind gets diverted. We don't remember the fear. We do not dwell in the fear. When we pray, our mind gets diverted and we feel things are fine. Don't think that your favorite God has come to help you. Even if one chants, 'Coca -Cola,

Coca-Cola, Coca-Cola,' one's mind will be diverted! One will not experience fear. But that is not the way to face fear. That is not the way to overcome fear.

The only way to overcome fear is to face it! Only then will we understand that death has no value. It is only we who give so much of importance to death. Please understand that death has power over us only because of our belief, our faith in it. It is just a matter of belief.

When we believe that death is terrifying, it becomes terrifying. It is like a mirror that faithfully reflects whatever we project on it. When a donkey sees itself in the mirror, what will it see? It will see a donkey, nothing else. Can it see anything else? In the same way, if we are totally afraid of death, then we will see only fear reflected back to us.

~ THE CYCLE OF LIFE AND DEATH

If we take a little time and look into our fear of death, we will see that it has the power to transform our life in the most positive way. We will realize that it is on our side and that it does not play a contradictory role in our lives and it is actually complementary to our lives.

Death is deep relaxation. It is the ultimate letting go. It is the dropping of the old and starting of the new. When our being recognizes that it cannot achieve what it wants to through this body, it decides to move on. This moving on, this passing over is what is called death.

When our brand new house becomes old after the passage of time, we either try to repair it or if that is too inconvenient and frustrating, we decide to sell the house and move into a new one. When we do this, do we feel that we are missing something? No! In the same way, when we feel that we have not lived our lives completely, fully in the way we wanted to, we leave this body to take a new one. We want to restart. God gives us a choice to start again, He gives us a boon and He blesses us. Our choice to start again is what is called death!

When we die, all that happens is that we rejuvenate our body and our mind. We take a fresh set of memories, a new setting, different set of relatives, and a new life. In other words, we take a new birth hoping to fulfill all our incomplete desires. We come back to finish whatever we left unaccomplished in the last birth. This choice given to us by God to start all over again is death.

However, without understanding this simple truth, we waste our whole lives doing everything possible to resist death. Once we add meditation to our lives, we start understanding our fears. Facing fear demystifies death. It is as if all the fog, all the snow and all the ice have been removed and we are able to see the sparkling water of understanding flowing clearly and beautifully. We start looking death in the eye.

When we face death, we see that it is nothing but life; because every moment we die, the next moment we are born. Death and birth are just cycles. If we die, we will be born; if we are born, we will die. We should understand that it is just a cycle. When this happens, we lose all fears. We start really living our lives. We start enjoying every breath that we take on planet Earth.

A small story:

The great philosopher Socrates was about to die. He had been forced by his detractors to drink hemlock, which is a deadly poison.
All his disciples were around him, mourning his impending death.
Socrates was his usual calm, composed self. Seeing his composure one of the younger disciples asked, 'You have been poisoned! You are about to die, and yet you are so relaxed, you are your usual self. Aren't you afraid of dying?'
Socrates looked up, smiled and said, 'Why should I be afraid of dying? Only two things can happen: either I will continue to exist in some form, in some name, in which case what is there to fear? Or I will cease to exist in any form, by any name, in which case who is there to fear? So either way there is nothing to fear!'

Beautiful, isn't it? Just courage and understanding can set us free of our deepest fears. Socrates was a rare kind of philosopher: He lived by his words. He practiced what he preached!

Modern physiologists claim that once every eighty days, all our blood cells change. Not a single one of the old cells remain. The whole lot, consisting of millions and millions of blood cells are replaced. In a total span of seven years, our entire body is replaced! It is a proven medical fact. We are not the same person that we were seven years ago. But does that fact upset us? Do we feel that we have lost something? No! The person who was there seven years ago is not there anymore. We are totally new people.

Understand that we are going through a continuous process of life and death. Yet, we are not disturbed. We are not frightened by this change that is happening within us. We don't feel like we are losing anything. Then why do we feel a sense of loss with death? That is because we have not faced it. We have not taken the time to study it, to understand it. That is why we feel so sick, so frightened of death.

When we face fear, the very concept of death disappears. Death becomes a God and Guru. Death is the master; master is death. Death teaches us beautiful things which life cannot teach us. Death is the greatest master. It empowers us; it sets us free from bondage. If this same understanding is applied to sex through meditation, then that also gets purified. It gets freed from our fantasies and dreams and flowers as ultimate love.

I always tell people: if one wants to spread anything all over the world one just has to put it up on a web site. It spreads immediately and reaches every corner of the globe. It becomes universal. Just add a 'dot com' and it becomes universal! Personal things become universal things. In the same way, add 'dot com' to your passion and it becomes 'com-passion'. When all our attention is covertly or overtly directed towards only one person, it is mere passion, lust. When we add the '.com' to lust it becomes universal, it becomes compassion. As long as it is directed towards one person, it is passion. When we give it to the whole world, it becomes compassion.

~ MEDITATION - THE LAST BIRTH AND THE LAST DEATH

When we meditate, our passion becomes compassion, our lust becomes love. Our dreams drop, our imagination gets burnt and our fantasies are destroyed. Our life experiences a total transformation. We understand life and sex in a different dimension. We penetrate death in a different dimension. When we add meditation to our daily living, we bridge life and death.

How can these three aspects - sex, death and meditation - become a single experience; how can they unite? First, we saw how they exist currently in our lives. Second, we saw what they can become when meditation is added to our lives. Now we will see how all three can lead to the same experience.

In sex, death and meditation, in all three, our mind experiences a gap, our intellect stops working and our being floods energy into our systems. Just for a moment, our mind stops working. Meditation gives us a glimpse of this mindless state. Actually we can reach the mindless state, access our innermost energy in three ways: through the physical, mental and the spiritual.

The physical way is through sex. Through sex also, we reach the mindless state. Just for a moment, we have a glimpse of the same joy, the same ecstasy. But it is not permanent. That is the problem. It is not permanent. It is *mithyananda*, not *nithyananda*. *Mithyananda* means ephemeral happiness which can disappear, which is not rooted in reality.

If we consciously penetrate death, we once again go through the outer-body experience. We will have a deep bodiless experience. When we enter into sex, death or meditation, we undergo the same boundariless experience; we reach the same exalted state.

Tantrics (people who practice *tantra*) use the body to reach the enlightened state through sex. *Vedantins* use the mind, enter through fear of death and reach enlightenment. Yogis work at the being level through meditation and reach enlightenment. In all three, logic is put aside. In sex also, we need to put our logic away. The man who is logical, who lives in his mind too much cannot really relate with the other. As I was mentioning earlier, living with a philosophy professor is the greatest possible hell on Earth!

Using the head too much does not allow us to relate with others. Whether it is sex, death or meditation, we need to drop our head; we have to become illogical. No matter how much we argue, death is not going to argue with us. Death is almost like a wife: she simply does, that's all! We may be great philosophers, convincing thousands and thousands of people in the world with our logic and arguments, but what happens inside the house? We can argue from morning till night, but in the end, we will see that the other does exactly what he or she want; they neither consult you nor give you any explanation.

Death also behaves in a similar manner. It never argues with us. We can plead, we can beg, we can cry for the postponement of our death. But no! Death will not wait to argue. Arguments or logic cannot be used with death. It is the same with meditation. The man who is logical can never meditate. He can never let go. In meditation also, we need to drop our logic.

Sex, death and meditation are similar types of experiences. In sex, we are born; in meditation, we are reborn. In death, we die; in meditation we die once and for all. In sex, we are born once. In death, we die once. In meditation, we do both. Both, death of the old and birth of the new happens in meditation. We become enlightened.

In sex, regular birth happens; in death, regular dying happens. In meditation, the last birth and the last death happen. We die as the Ego is the last death. Our taking birth as an enlightened person is the last birth. Our last death and last birth: nirvana is the last nightmare; Enlightenment is the last dream. So also with meditation, our last death happens and our last birth happens.

When we add meditation to our lives, we see that both life and death are bridged. If we are wise, we will add meditation to bridge both, to unite both. When we do this, both become one. As long as we don't have this bridge, both are separate cities. When we bridge them, they are no longer two separate cities, they become one.

When we bridge life and death with meditation, we experience a totally different way of living. We experience the ultimate birth and ultimate death. Please understand very clearly, meditation enriches our death and enriches our sex. It enriches our leaving and our living.

Meditation is the way to unite, to communicate and to commune between birth and death. It transforms our lives. If we bring meditation between birth and death, it makes our lives worthy. Otherwise, it is just one more cycle in the great cycle of our personal evolution.

Ramana Maharishi says beautifully, 'If we wake up from our dreams, we come out of our dreams. If we don't wake up, we just dream, fall asleep, dream again, fall asleep again and dream again. The same cycle continues.'

In the same way, when we become enlightened, we come out of this dream of life and death. Otherwise, the cycle of birth and death goes on continuously. Until we wake up, until we meditate, the cycle of life and death will go on without our conscious awareness.

Someone asked me, 'Master, why is it that on most tombstones in graveyards we see: Born on this date, died on this date? I told him that nothing worth mentioning happens in between, that's why!

In many of our lives, only our birth and death are worth mentioning. Nothing else worthwhile happens. If we add meditation, then something really worth mentioning happens in our lives between birth and death; something so worthwhile that it can transform our very living.

Add meditation as a bridge between birth and death. If we miss meditation, we miss the real dimension of our life. Meditation is not meant to be just a part of our lives. It is not something we do for half an hour and forget for the next twenty-three and half-hours. It is meant to transform our whole life. Please understand that meditation is not a luxury; it is a necessity! Do not find excuses to postpone meditation.

Meditation is like a bright torch; it is the light with which we can explore all the dimensions of our lives. When we do this, we start understanding each and every dimension in a new way. That is why I tell you to build this bridge, so that you will understand both banks of the river. When we build the bridge of meditation, life, death and meditation all meet and merge in the river of Existence, the river of *Brahman*, God, the Divine, Eternal Bliss. So I request you all to construct this bridge, to touch both the banks of your life with courage and understanding.

May this bridge of meditation not only help unite the two seemingly opposing banks, but also help you reach the experience that all the three lead to: enlightenment, eternal bliss, *nithya-ananda*.

~ Questions and Answers:

Is *Kundalini* awakening the only way to enlightenment?

Actually when we become enlightened, the *kundalini* (energy centre located at the navel) awakens automatically. The *kundalini* getting awakened is not the only way; it is one way, but not the only way. There are so many other techniques. It is actually vice versa. When we get enlightened, the *kundalini* automatically gets awakened. But to reach the enlightened state, there are so many other paths. So we can reach through any technique. But once we reach that enlightened state, the *kundalini* automatically awakens.

What is the root of all evil?

This question is the root of all evil! The questioning mind, the intellectual mind which continuously questions is the root of all evil!

Why do we do prostrations and touch the feet of the master or God? Is it not a de-humanizing experience?

It is the only humanizing experience. If we don't touch the feet of the God or the master, we will be touching the feet of our own ego. If we don't follow God or our master, we will be following our own ego.

People come and ask me, 'Master, why should we chant God's name?' I tell them that there is no need to chant God's name. Why should we chant? If we don't chant Rama or Krishna, we will be chanting 'coca-cola, coca-cola', or our wife's name, that's all! If we chant the Divine name, we will not be chanting the other things. If we don't chant this, we will be chanting that; that's all. That is what one youngster asked me, 'Why should we chant *Rama, Rama, Krishna, Krishna*? I hate all this stuff, master!' I told him, it is alright. If we feel comfortable chanting something else, do that!

If we don't touch the feet of God, the feet of the masters, we will be touching our own ego's feet. There are only two options for us: either we listen to the master or we listen to the ego. Master is the man who has already achieved eternal bliss, *nithya-ananda*. So if we follow him, we will get that state. As for our ego, what it has achieved and towards what it is leading us, we already know! If we are quite happy, comfortable, content, blissful in the path in which our ego is leading us, then we can touch our ego's feet, nothing wrong. If we are happy, ecstatic, blissful with our ego, then we can follow our ego, touch the feet of our ego; there is nothing wrong. If we are a little uncomfortable, if we want to change, then the time has come to follow the master's path.

There are only two things: master and the mind. If we follow the master, we cannot follow the mind; if we follow the mind, we cannot follow the master. If we touch the feet of the master, we will not touch the feet of the mind; if we don't touch the feet of the master, we will be touching the feet of the mind.

That is why there is a beautiful word *namaha* in Sanskrit. When people touch the feet of the master, they say *namaha*. It means, 'Not mine, I am not the 'I', the 'I' and 'mine' are surrendered at your feet.' The 'I' and 'mine' are surrendered at the feet of the master or God. So touching the feet of the God or the master is the only humanizing experience. If we don't, we will be following our senses, we will be following our mind, which is the greatest dehumanizing experience. We drop from our divinity to become animals.

So touching the master's feet will make us human beings; imbibing his teachings will make us Divine. This is the only humanizing experience that can happen in our lives. Of course, I personally don't encourage touching the feet or doing the *pada-puja* (anointing the feet of the master). But now, I am explaining from the philosophical point of view.

Is learning about our past lives a good way of helping resolve some of the issues in our present life? If it were, would you be able to uncover my past life and tell me what it was like?

Learning about our past lives is a really good way of resolving some of our issues. We do this in our initial level meditation program. This meditation technique, the cleansing of the *chakra,* has given experiences or a glimpse of past lives for many participants. It clears it without you knowing it. It clears it at a very deep level. But if I start teling you about your past lives, it will only add chaos to your present lives. Even with present life memories, you are unable to live peacefully! Imagine if I open up your past life memories! There is no need. What needs to surface and leave you will leave you through our meditation itself.

People are afraid of enlightenment as much as they are afraid of death; am I correct?

You asked the right question. We are undergoing the last nightmare. *Nirvana* is the last nightmare. A devotee questioned Ramana Maharishi, 'How can seeing the master help us to wake up or become enlightened, *Bhagavan*?' Ramana Maharishi replied, 'The master is a *simha-swapna* (dream or nightmare of a lion) for us. He is a nightmare for us. If we experience a nightmare when we are asleep, we wake up with a start! If we see an elephant chasing us, or a snake biting us in our dream, what happens? We wake up from our dream. In the same way, the master is a *simha-swapna;* he just frightens us out of our unconscious way of living.'

We can wake up in two ways: either through a dream of deep desire or a dream of deep fear! If in our dream we see someone whom we have wanted to meet for a long time, the moment we go to grab him or her, we will wake up! Just at the point when our desire is about to be fulfilled, we wake up! It is the same with fear also. If we have a nightmare, a dream that totally shakes us, frightens us, we wake up before we actually die in the dream!

Dreams related to sex wake us up; dreams related to fear wake us up. Both wake us up. In both the cases, we wake up to the conscious state. In the same way, the master also uses two techniques to wake us up from our long slumber. He creates in us the greed for bliss. He is continuously blissful, ecstatic. We feel envious of his state. We feel a deep, disturbing jealousy. Many people tell me, 'Master, we may or may not understand half the things you speak. All we know is that we feel very jealous of your blissful state. You are so busy meeting your devotees, listening to their problems, looking into the organizational work, traveling and yet you remain fresh and joyful all the time!'

Yes, the master creates a tremendous greed in you. He shows you that something more is possible; that you are capable of much more. The master is a tree and you are a seed. He shows you that you can become a tree. He proves your potentiality. He is the certificate or the authority of the state in which you can flower, in which you can blossom. He continuously creates the greed in us to reach that state. He awakens us so we may become enlightened. For some people who do not respond to greed, he creates a deep fear of logic: you are in hell, the seventh hell. The desire of seventh heaven and the fear of seventh hell are created just to wake us up, slap our face! Wake up! You are Buddha. That's all!

The death penalty was introduced in the American constitution not long ago. Now the government executes people who murder someone. Is this the correct thing to do spiritually? Would it help the overall development of the society? Or would it inflict more negative emotions in an atmosphere of pain?

Of course, we are no one to comment or criticize the law of a place. But from the spiritual point of view, I can give you a small explanation. The concept of 'an eye for an eye' is: if someone takes your eye and you take his eye in return, he will take one more of your eyes and you will take one more of his eyes. Then, his followers will take one of your follower's eyes. If this 'eye for an eye' goes on continuously, where will it end? The whole world will become blind! It will end only in the blindness of the entire world. So an eye for an eye is not the preferred mode of retribution. We are no one to comment on the government's reason to do so. We cannot criticize the political structure or the constitution of a country. They have their own reasons. But from the spiritual stand point, death for death is not advocated. Transformation should happen at the individual level and it is perfectly possible for peace to prevail.

Regarding the meditation that we did yesterday, I am not clear about what was said at the end. You said *Aum*, and then something; could you please say it clearly so I can know what the chant is?

When the meditation ended, I chanted the peace mantra: *Aum shanti, shanti, shantihi. Shanti* means peace. That is the vibration which creates peace in us, which creates silence in us. It is the bridge that can connect us with Existence.

While in a deep meditative state, you may be in another plane. You need to come down to this plane. Suddenly bringing you back may give you a shock or a jolt. It may shake you. You should be brought back in a very loving, beautiful way. It is like when babies are delivered, these modern nurses treat babies roughly. They give a stinging slap to the tender bodies of the babies! It gives them a terrible shock. Of course, we should make them cry, there is nothing wrong with that. We should make them cry and only then, will they start breathing. But it need not be done in such a rude manner.

They are not received with love or in a welcoming mood when they come to planet Earth. When we are born on planet Earth, our mind is very fresh, pure, and clean. The first moment of a baby's life is very crucial to the manner in which it will respond to the world later in life. This moment will be imprinted forever in it's being. The emotion of that single moment will decide the way in which that individual will live his life. That is why, with a few exceptions, all of humanity is still reacting to the manner in which they were welcomed to planet Earth!

We live our lives protecting ourselves, defending ourselves from pain. We close ourselves to all possibilities. Now we are trying to work with a technique of painless delivery so that babies will be received with love. They will be welcomed in a gentle manner in a fragrant atmosphere with beautiful music.

When newborns are received with deep love, in a caring manner, they will carry this love and the feeling of giving themselves to others all through their lives. Please understand that the impression received at birth is carried till the very end of our lives.

Similarly, when we come out of meditation, we are like babies. We need to be brought down to the realities of this world in a gentle, loving manner. A small bridge is necessary to connect us to this plane so that we can carry the joy, the peace and the silence of our meditation with us twenty-four hours a day throughout our lives. That is why, *'Aum, shanti, shanti, shantihi'* is chanted at the end of every meditation.

May we have the knowledge and the experience of eternal bliss, *nithya ananda*!

Epilogue

As this book was being compiled from a few of Master's discourses, his father passed away while he was delivering a discourse on Ashtavakra Gita to a packed audience in Bangalore on 12 November 2005. Only a handful in the discourse hall knew what had happened since Master continued with the discourse and the blessing session followed without missing a beat, after he was informed of his father's death.

The following article is a rendering by a disciple who along with a few other healers and ordained teachers (acharyas) accompanied Master to Tiruvannamalai where his father Sri Arunachalananda had attained enlightenment and left the body, what we call Maha Samadhi.

This article describes the way our Master walked his talk. Death indeed was a liberation, a celebration, a continuum.

In the timeless Katopanishad, Nachiketa asks Yama, Lord of Death:

When a person dies, there comes this doubt: he exists, say some; no he does not, say others. Teach me the Truth, that's the boon I ask thee!

The Master answers this without words through a profound event described in the following pages.

Death: The Ultimate Liberation

It was the third and final day of the *Ashtavakra Gita* discourse in Bangalore.

The topic: 'Enlightenment-Have It!' The hall was packed to overflowing. There was pin drop silence as the young Master expounded so authoritatively on the *sutras* of the boy sage - Ashtavakra. The mesmerized audience listened to the flow of words suddenly interrupted by a coughing bout.

Master asked for water, drank and continued talking.

There was another interruption. Ayya (Secretary to Master for the mission in India) came up on to the stage, went behind Master's seat and whispered something. Master covered the mike with his hand, listened calmly with a facial expression that conveyed 'I'll take care' or something to that effect. The discourse resumed. Then to the audience's utter consternation, Master gestured for Ayya to come on stage. More whispered exchanges followed. There was stillness, finality about Master's body language. Ayya left, the talk continued and finished. The effect of the speech was electrifying. No one left their seats; spontaneous applause; long serpentine queue for Master's blessings.

I sat in the balcony watching the flow of events. Little did I know that one soul had already taken the offer of enlightenment.

The Master is compassion incarnate. He blessed each and every one of those who sought his grace. As the long line of people was shortening, I went down to the entrance to take my allotted place. Just then Ayya came and said, '*Ma*, Master's father has attained *Maha Samadhi*. All of us are leaving for Tiruvannamalai as soon as Master finishes. Please round up all the *acharyas* (teachers) and healers and gather them in one place. At no point in time should our body language reveal what I have just conveyed to you. Master wants us all to remain calm and act with spiritual maturity.'

That set the tone for the unimaginable series of events that followed. Very smoothly Master's car moved away with his mother beside him in the centre seat and a few others occupying the rear seat. Mini buses were arranged for us, most not knowing why we were leaving. The unknowing ones were delighted by the turn of events. They were travelling out of Bangalore and would be in Master's company.

That was enough!

When we reached Tiruvannamalai, one of the ashramites stopped the bus, clambered down and picked up some fresh garlands for all of us to place on the coffin. In the wee hours of the morning on the thirteenth of November, the bus stopped at the entrance to Rajarajan Street where Master's maternal grandparents lived. A passing thought struck me that the young ***Raja***shekaran had lived in ***Raja***rajan street and was destined to be a ***Raja***sannyasi - royalty in the manner born (*Raja* meaning king). It looked like Existence had planned very meticulously.

The orchestration was truly exquisite!

All of us got down quietly and walked solemnly in single file into the house. Master was sitting on the veranda with some male relatives. He was radiating a serene calmness. The minute he saw us, he remarked to the people beside him, 'For the first time I am seeing these fellows really serious.' He then told us, 'Go inside. Pay your respects. Be with my mother. See to it that no one disturbs her. I don't want anyone wailing and weeping and creating any scenes.'

We stepped into the hall and saw a lot of people seated there. Just to the left of the main doorway was the glass coffin. One after the other, in silence, we placed the garlands on the coffin and paid our respects. I looked at the face and found it to be utterly calm. It echoed the final relaxation. Somehow, I couldn't connect the fact that this inert mass I was looking at was a living person to whom I had spoken just two days ago in the *ashram*. I had bid him goodbye and said that we would see each other during the Jayanti celebrations. In his usual manner, he invited me over to his place for the *Karthigai Deepam* festival... *ellarum vaango* (everybody come). *Karthigai Deepam* is a festival of lights exclusive to Tiruvannamalai. Scores of people travel from world over to be here at that time.

Yes, everyone came but not for the festival. Little did we know that we had been invited for a celebration, the likes of which we had never seen in our lives. I found the atmosphere very strange. I couldn't put my finger on it. Then it suddenly dawned on me that no one was crying! Everyone was sitting quietly. I had witnessed too many deaths in the family. The ambience had always been one of great grief; wailing and shouting and calling out to the departed one was the rule rather than the exception.

I had no doubt in my mind that the Master was the single controlling factor here.

We all sat around Lokanayaki Amma (Master's mother) who was an inspiration to watch. She was sitting on the ground, next to the sofa on which Master sat. There was an air of innocence and dignity in her demeanor. She aligned her wishes to whatever Master said. She exhibited a total childlike trust in him. As she so simply and beautifully put it: *Saami ennodu irrukumpodu vera enna ma ennakku venum? Avar ellamay patthuparu, ma.* (When Master Himself is with me, what more can I ask for? He will take care of everything, *ma.*)

She showed a high level of spiritual maturity that is rare for a person, especially a woman born and brought up in a small, closed society.

I understood why Master had chosen her to be his mother. He had mentioned somewhere that energy attracts Higher Beings and makes them act as the spiritual incubator for all Masters when they descend on planet Earth. In a similar way, I felt Amma, due to her extreme innocence and unshakeable spiritual strength was the womb, the incubator that had radiated the innate capacity to receive and nurture Master's exalted energy.

The whole day was suffused with an air of spiritual fervor. Even as people were trooping in to pay their respects, all the *brahmacharis* looked ascetically resplendent as they performed various *pujas* with Master's presence and participation. There was *Guru puja, Vraja homa, Nithya kirtans, Arti* and a lot of input from the Master Himself.

As Master explained, 'When Ayya came to the stage and informed me that my father was no more, I paused for a while and related to the energy. I very clearly saw that just before actual death, father had gone into an enlightened state and had stayed there for at least twenty one minutes. He had attained *maha samadhi.* Then he relaxed beautifully into the all pervading Consciousness. I told Ayya to relax and carry on with the necessary arrangements. In those few moments of relating, I had done whatever had to be done at the initial stage for the soul to move on.

Now let me take care of all these people who have come here for my blessings. They too need me.'

Only a person in the *Paramahamsa* state can be so compassionately detached and available unconditionally at all times for those who seek him, no matter the nature of the existing situation. In those few moments, the teachings of Ashtavakra - we are by our very nature unattached, renounced, liberated; we are the all pervading, witnessing consciousness - had been expressed through the Master's body language.

The profound Truths of the Scriptures have to be lived. Here before our eyes was a living example for all of us - devotees, disciples, healers and *acharyas* were being shown what it really meant to practice what one preaches. Masters do not teach. Their very life is the teaching. If we are alert and awake when around the Master, we can learn within moments what years of pouring over great philosophies cannot teach us.

Every now and then, Master would go out, sit in the veranda, watch the arrangements being made to receive people and speak with his father's relatives and friends in their moments of reminiscing.

He said with great fondness: by his own right my father was a V.I.P. (Very Important Person) in this town because of his innate generosity of spirit and his helpful nature. He had a great fan following. He was so considerate to everyone. Even the last moments he spent on planet Earth were with great consideration, just as he did not disturb me when I was a mere boy on the spiritual path, so too in death he chose to cause me the least disturbance. In my very busy schedule, I am relatively free for the next three days. He chose to leave his body only now! He could have gone when I was in America or during the *Ananda Ula* (tour of Tamilnadu). What would have happened to all the programs, all the arrangements? A beautiful soul! I have blessed him with the ultimate gift of enlightenment. He has left his body smoothly, without any pain. He is relaxed and relating with me. *Amma, nee kavalai padadhey, naa pathikirain*. (Amma, dont worry. I will take care.)

So saying, Master stood up, walked to the glass coffin and very lovingly, with a beautiful smile on his face blessed his father's body and energy. He repeated this often, throughout the day.

The gentry of Tiruvannamalai were exposed to the joyous dignity of death.

Hearing him talk and watching his utterly relaxed, confident, authoritative body language, I realized we were sitting in a live classroom. He was living the truths that he had spoken of on many occasions, especially during the ASP and NSP. He was showing us the way in which we should receive death, the way we should handle the dead and the living. No book can ever give us this kind of understanding, this kind of confidence. I understood why he was particularly careful on maintaining a deeply joyous atmosphere; why he was insistent that no one should weep or wail.

As far as my understanding goes, when the soul leaves the body it is essential that the atmosphere is light, suffused with spiritual understanding, awareness and a mood of deep celebration. Then we make it easier for the soul to move on smoothly to the next dimension.

This is the greatest gift of love we can give to anyone; this is the ultimate act of selflessness.

When we cry, when we grieve, we create such a heavy atmosphere that the soul struggles to leave. We create an obstruction. This is the greatest act of cruelty that we can commit. We suffer from the misconception that if we weep, we are telling the departed one how much we love him/her. Actually, if we look deeply and honestly within ourselves, we will see that we are crying for the loss, the void that the person's death has caused in our lives. If we really understand that death is the climax of life and not the end of life, we too will celebrate with that understanding.

Then where is the room for tears?

When evening arrived that day, *sandhya arti* (an offering of lit camphor) was performed to the sound of the tinkling bells and the rhythmic

clapping of the gathering. Everyone participated with great fervor. I was sitting next to the coffin. Each time my gaze turned to my left, I was looking directly at the face of the departed soul. I was surprised by the fact that at no time was I ever disturbed by this physical proximity to the body. In fact, most often than not we even forgot that the body was there though it was placed in the centre of the room. It did not hold centre stage. There was no exhibition of grief or any trace of morbidity to keep us focused on the body.

I realized that as the Master was constantly keeping the group occupied with some aspect of spirituality, the mind was diverted from its habituated pattern of responding to such situations. Our energies, instead of being tight and confined to our boundaries through fear and grief, were expanding and relating to the high level of enlightened energy present in the room. The moment of death can be a process of deep alchemy for the dying and the living. Since this blessed soul had attained *samadhi,* the energy it was radiating combined with the high vibrations that the Master exuded had the power to transform something in all those tuned to it. And that is exactly what the Master was making us do.

He did not want us to miss the huge opportunity that Existence was offering us.

In between all these extraordinary activities, Master kept the normalcy of the day-to-day activities going. We went out for breakfast, came back, drank coffee that was served with polite hospitality to our bodies and even did the *giri-valam* (circumambulating the Arunachala hill). In short, the ordinariness of day-to-day life carried on. This in no way showed disrespect to the departed soul. On the contrary, it showed an extremely mature understanding that death is one more event in our

as simple as changing our old worn clothes for something

anging is death. If while living we had learnt the art of ... then we would carry the same attitude while dying. If we wish to die well, all we have to do is to live well, live fully, moment to moment, as if each moment is our last one; then there will be no room for regret. We will have the spiritual understanding that death is neither frightening nor exciting as some naively think. It is simply a fact of life which gives us a great opportunity for the most profound and beneficial inner experiences to come about.

It carries with it the potentiality to be the moment of Final Illumination.

Early next morning, around 5.30 a.m., we gathered in the main hall. Master asked that the body be given its final bath and draped in *kavi vastra* (saffron clothes). At that moment I remembered: once when Master was coming back from a tour of the South, his father told the eldest son, who too had come to visit the ashram, *seekaram vaa da... sami varadukulla nambba kazhambalam paatarna nambazhayum samiyara panniduvaru* (Come quickly. Let us leave before Master arrives. If he sees us, he will make us also *sannyasis*!) It looked like Existence had a great sense of humor. Master had the last laugh. I am sure that Master's father, Sri Nithya Arunachalananda would have joined in the laughter.

I noticed that there was no change in the physical condition of the body. Death had arrived on 12th evening and now it was the morning of the 14th. The body looked exactly as it had been on the first day that we had seen it. It was kept on ice; yet there was no change, considering the heat of Tiruvannamalai and that the glass coffin was not the most sophisticated. The face radiated the same sereneness. There was no body odour though the use of *agarbhattis* and room fresheners had stopped.

I mused silently: was it because of Master's energy field? Or was it due to the vibrations of all the *pujas* and *artis* that were being performed at regular intervals? Or to the fact that the group energy was so profoundly calm and elevating? Perhaps it was a direct reflection of the *samadhi* state into which Sri Arunachalananada had entered.

Before leaving the body, the individuated ego with all its sense-residues had been transformed and purified at the moment of the final exit. There was no odour; only the lightness and bliss of the liberated soul suffused the air that we breathed. It could be all these aspects acting together. I honestly don't know. This was not the time to seek clarifications. That understanding would arise automatically when the time was right, without any kind of seeking or prompting. And of course, my ego never got tired of musing.

Once all the necessary formalities were done, Master asked everyone who was not a healer or an *acharya* (teacher) to pay their respects and leave the room. Then, closing the doors and the windows firmly, He asked Nithya Kirtanananda to play the ananda-darshan music. The room exploded to the beat of *bomma bomma, tha thaiya thaiya thaka* with everyone singing and clapping. Master threw his hands in the air and clapped, throwing tremendous energy all around. There was a great buildup of heat in the closed room. Then, he placed his *ajna* (third eye) on his father's *ajna*. He uttered '*maha vakya, tatvam asi, tatvam asi, tatvam asi, aham brahmasmi, aham brahmasmi, aham brahmasmi.*' Intense energy transfer must have taken place. One cannot even begin to understand its meaning. Then with absolute grace he removed his turban and put it on his father's head; then he placed *rudraksh mala* around his neck. Then keeping to the beat of the cosmic rhythm, he jumped gracefully and nimbly on to the low table on which his father's body was laid. A few pulse beats later, with exquisite dexterity, he placed the big toe of his right foot on his father's *ajna* ever so gently and threw up his hands in utter ecstasy.

That moment is frozen in the memory. He was both the destroyer and the creator. Whatever I had heard, read and studied about Shiva was happening in front of me. The sketches, the sculptures, the paintings were coming alive. The whole moment was deeply *tantric* in its intensity. Something in me just gave way. I felt an ecstatic connectivity. Shiva was no longer a mere concept for me. I realized that the updated version of Shiva was my own dear Master. It just blew my mind. Something in me died forever for something else to bloom.

Later, just before the doors were opened to let people in, one of the healers echoed the feeling in all our hearts when he said: Master, if this is how death is going to be, then I am ready to die right now!

The next moments were all about hi(s)tory being created in Tiruvannamalai. For the very first time, women were allowed to accompany the funeral procession to the cremation area. The bier was lifted on to the flower-bedecked vehicle. With Master leading the way, women singing the beautifully evocative devotional lyrics of the *Arunachala Aksharamana Maalai* song accompanied it on its last earthly journey. The most poignant and unbelieving part of this moment was the fact that Lokanayaki Amma, the wife of the departed soul was walking alongside, rhythmically clapping her hands to the beat of the devotional song - an expression of implicit trust, of inner steel, of dignified grace.

When we reached the cremation area, Master informed us that this was the land gifted by Amma's father to start a Nithyananda Dhyanapeetam centre. He revealed to the gathering that the first person to attend the NSP and get enlightened before leaving the body was his father. It was only befitting that the body of a realized soul should be cremated here. When the pyre was readied, the mortal remains of Sri Sri Sri Nithya Arunachalananda was placed on it. The way the body was positioned was truly symbolic. At one end was the sacred Arunachala; at the other end was Master in the formless and in the form.

Can anyone ask for greater protection than this?

As the final moments arrived for the curtain to be drawn, people were given flowers to offer at the feet of the body one last time. Then, Master informed the gathered crowd that as a *sannyasi* (renunciate), he couldn't perform the last rites, but as a *Guru* (Master), it was his

responsibility to conduct the rites of passage for his disciple. Master recalled that when he had asked his father what kind of help he needed, his father had answered simply: *Swami irunda podum.* (If you are there, that is enough). Master said, 'At that moment, he became my disciple.' That complete, total trust is enough. Nothing else is needed.

Master also declared that in future, the 12th of November, every year - the death anniversary of Sri Nithya Arunachalananda will be celebrated as the day of Enlightened Souls, in memory of all those who attain enlightenment and leave the body under the Master's grace. He promised no matter where his disciples died, his energy would be there to perform the last rites. With such an amazing promise thundering into our very beings, the last lingering fear of death if any, just melted away.

This was a promise from none other than Existence itself.

As his father's energy had travelled directly from a conscious state to a super conscious one without slipping into the unconscious coma state, and had remained in that exalted level for 21 minutes, he had become enlightened. Therefore he could not be treated normally. Also since he had been conferred with the *Andhima Sannyas* (final renunciation and enlightenment) by the Master prior to cremation, the body had to be cremated with all the honours that are conferred on enlightened souls.

It was like a spiritual military salute of honour to a courageous warrior. Just before the pyre was lit, Master called his mother and brothers, gave them each a sandalwood log to place on the mortal remains of the energy that had been a husband and father for so many years. There was a finality to that act. Then with the shouts of 'Sri Sri Sri Sri Sri Nithya Arunacahlananda *Ki Jai*' - hail to the departed soul - filling the air, Master performed the *arati*, lit the funeral pyre and consigned it to the flames, with flowing grace and compassion.

The last cameo shot that I remember is of Master putting his arm around his mother and hugging her to his side acknowledging her trusting innocence, spiritual strength and courage.

He stood tall with his biological family around him as Son, Brother, Master, God.

I express my love and respect to each and everyone reading this. It was our deep longing to share this experience with every one of you.

In Nithyananda,
- MNM

Appendix

It was under the glow of the spiritual magnet Arunachala in the energy center of Tiruvannamalai in South India, that Paramahamsa was born - as Rajasekharan, to Arunachalam and Lokanayaki, on 1 Jan 1978. The family astrologer predicted that he would be a king amongst holy men. At the age of 3, Paramahamsa was associated with Yogiraj Raghupati Maharaj, yoga guru, who took him through rigorous training and prepared his body with apparent foresight into the energy explosion that was going to happen in the young body. From the age of 5, Paramahamsa took to deity worship with great passion. He showed profound commitment to the rituals he practiced with the deities. Just a few years later, he came in touch with Mataji Kuppammal, a deeply pious lady who initiated him into *Vedanta* and *Tantra*. He started his scriptural learning at a young age. He encountered many mystics from the town of Tiruvannamalai and received many teachings from them. He had his first deep spiritual experience at the age of 12 when he was sitting on a rock on the Arunachala hillock. He had a 360 degree panoramic vision and experienced becoming one with everything around

The earliest picture of Paramahamsa in meditation taken when he was 10 years old

him. This experience inspired him further to forge ahead in his journey inwards.

nithyananda meditating in Arunachala

To Paramahamsa, academics was just another incident in life. With only the attention he gave in classes at school and polytechnic, he passed all his grades with distinction. He obtained a diploma degree in Mechanical Engineering from a leading private polytechnic in Tamilnadu. At the age of 17, he left home driven by the irresistible urge to jump into the real life that he was seeking. He wandered through the length and breadth of India and Nepal, studying Eastern metaphysical Sciences at the feet of many masters and mystics. He visited many great shrines ranging from the Himalayan ranges in the North to Kanyakumari in the South, from Dwaraka in the West to Ganga Sagar in the East. He endured intense meditation and other austerities and attained inner bliss the state of *nithyananda* or eternal bliss - at the age of 22. Rajasekharan became Paramahamsa Nithyananda.

Flagging off construction on mission site

Guided by Divine Vision, on 1 Jan 2003, Paramahamsa set up his mission headquarters in Bangalore, India in the land of a mystical and sacred banyan tree.

Today, Paramahamsa Nithyananda is an inspiring personality for millions of people worldwide. From his experience of the Truth, he has formulated and gifted the *Technology of Bliss* to every individual.

His methods empower us to be physically and mentally fit individuals with sound spiritual strength. Millions of people around the world have experienced radical transformation through his techniques in short periods of time.

He gives the tools to live a creative and productive life guided by intuition and intelligence rather than by intellect or instinct. He shows the way to excellence in the outer world and radiance in the inner world both at the same time. His programs teach one to fall into the natural space known as meditation.

Paramahamsa says, 'Meditation is the master key that can bring success in the material world and deep fulfillment in your space within.' His powerful techniques and processes that comprise the meditation programs, help the flowering and explosion of individual consciousness in short periods of time.

Paramahamsa works with scientists and researchers world over to record the mystic phenomena through scientific data. He intrigues the world of medical science with results from his own neurological system. From the astounding observations, scientists feel that the potential for altering the rates and progression of diseases like heart ailments, cancer, arthritis, alcoholism etc. are beginning to look achievable.

Life Bliss Foundation is Paramahamsa's worldwide movement for meditation and transformation. Established in the year 2003 and now spanning over 1000 centers in 33 countries, the Life Bliss Foundation transforms humanity through transformation of the individual.

Sacred Banyan tree, Bidadi ashram, India

Nithyananda Meditation Academies (NMAs) worldwide serve as spiritual laboratories where inner growth is profound and outer growth is a natural consequence. These academies are envisioned to be a place and space to explore and explode, through a host of activities, from meditation to science. They offer quantum spirituality, where material and spiritual worlds merge and create blissful living; where creative intelligence stems from deep consciousness.

Hyderabad ashram, India

Los Angeles ashram, USA

Many projects are in development at the various academies worldwide; and new academies are being established to provide services in varied fields to humanity at large.

A diverse range of meditation programs and social services are offered worldwide through the Foundation. Free energy healing through the Nithya Spiritual Healing system, free education to youth, encouragement to art and culture, *satsangs* (spiritual circles), personality development programs, corporate programs, free medical camps and eye surgeries, free meals at all ashrams worldwide, a one-year residential spiritual training program in India, an in-house *gurukul* system of learning for children and many more services are offered around the world.

Seattle ashram, USA

Salem ashram, India

Ananda Sevaks of the Nithya Dheera Seva Sena (NDSS) volunteer force comprising growing numbers of dedicated volunteers around the world, support the mission with great enthusiasm.

A number of new ashrams and centers are being set up around the world.

Colombus ashram, Ohio, USA

Contact us:

USA:

Life Bliss Foundation
9720 Central Avenue
Montclair
California 91763
USA
Ph.: 1-909-625-1400
Email: programs@lifebliss.org

INDIA:

Nithyananda Dhyanapeetam
Nithyanandapuri
Kallugopahalli
Mysore Road, Bidadi
Bangalore - 562 109
Karnataka
INDIA
Ph.: 91 +80 65591844
Telefax: 91 +80 27202084
Email: mail@dhyanapeetam.org

Visit our web site www.nithyananda.org for more information.

Suggested for further reading...

Life Bliss Foundation offers many volumes of books and CDs across 23 languages. They are tools of blissful living for any type of person. A few of the books are listed here:

! Guaranteed Solutions for sex, fear, worry etc.
! Nithyananda Vol. 1 of Paramahamsa Nithyananda's biography
! Meditation is for you
! Bliss is the path and the goal
! The only way out is IN
! Rising in love with the Master
! Bhagavad Gita series
! 'Why' series
! A to Z 'click' books
! Uncommon answers to common questions
! Open the door…Let the breeze in!

To purchase books & other items

visit www.lifeblissgalleria.com
or contact us at www.nithyananda.org

To view online video clips of Paramahamsa's discourses around the world, visit: www.youtube.com/lifeblissfoundation